MONTESSORI

HER METHOD AND THE MOVEMENT
WHAT YOU NEED TO KNOW

Edited by R. C. OREM

Capricorn Books

G. P. PUTNAM'S SONS, NEW YORK

Copyright © 1974 by R. C. Orem

*SBN: 399-11362-2
Library of Congress Catalog Card Number: 74-83094*

PUBLISHED IN THE UNITED STATES OF AMERICA

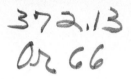
For Louis Orem

MY BROTHER

ACKNOWLEDGMENTS

During the preparation of this book the members and staffs of approximately one hundred Montessori organizations and facilities extended their cooperation. These organizations and facilities included Montessori associations, societies, and institutes—international, national, regional, state, city, and local; Montessori schools and programs; teacher training courses; conferences, seminars, and workshops; parent groups, study groups. Although a compilation of individual acknowledgments is not feasible, perhaps the book itself will serve as a fitting acknowledgment to the contributions of Montessorians too numerous to mention.

Contents

SECTION IV

APPENDICES

Foreword

Stones for Breakfast
by Russell Kirk

Maria Montessori understood the imagination of children, and their creative powers. And, as this latest book by R. C. Orem reminds us, she taught us how to direct that imagination and those powers toward what T. S. Eliot calls "the high dream." Bad schooling for little boys and girls betrays them lifelong to "the low dream."

Permit me an illustrative anecdote. Up where I dwell, snowdrifts persist into April. About two years ago, upon the first day of spring, my three little daughters began to gambol: Persephone had waked their imagination and their talents for creation.

Like the beasts that perish, little children become intoxicated by the coming of spring. On our first warm and bright morning, my Monica (aged three), Cecilia (aged two) and Felicia (aged eleven months) could not be kept indoors. Though still in their pajamas, they burst outside and commenced to caper and sing.

Monica, emulated enthusiastically by Cecilia, began piling stones on our back steps. "Stones for breakfast!" she shouted. "We're going to have stones for breakfast tonight!" Not to be outdone in fantasy, Cecilia tried to feed pebbles to Felicia, exclaiming "Tones for b'eckfast!" Felicia endeavored to escape from her father's clutch and crawl down to the wan grass.

"Hush!" said Monica. "I hear a bird!" Cecilia spied out a venturesome insect. Only my prompt exertions prevented Felicia from devouring the pebbles in earnest.

As the years pass, too many of the rising generation are given not bread, but a stone. In the spring of life, nearly everything is wondrous. The fortunate are those who, like Maria Montessori, never lose their sense of wonder: who subsist upon the bread of spirit, and laugh at the stones of dullness and materialism. It is a good omen that a very little girl should be fanciful enough to set out stones for breakfast; that quality may save her, years later, from mistaking stones for bread.

With my three playful daughters, that first spring morning, I enjoyed one of those moments in which time and the timeless intersect—a glimpse of immortality. Heaven may be perpetual spring. Those people who fail to perceive timeless moments are the prisoners of time and circumstance. It is only by transcending the ravenous ego, and sharing joy with others, that we realize our true and enduring selves. Hell, I suspect, is imprisonment within the ego, through the perpetual winter of discontent.

Monica, Cecilia, and Felicia, like all children, someday must put away childish things, and must come to know the ills to which flesh is heir. Yet the resurrection of flesh and spirit is promised to those who become as little children.

Evil, too, is childish—in the sense that the evil person is trapped in the selfishness, the wrath, and the hasty appetites which are childish vices. The evil man is one who never has learned to order his soul. Yet in learning to restrain and to discipline themselves, little girl-daughters need not lose that love of proliferating life which breaks out in spring. To the end, wonder and joy can be found by those whose senses truly perceive; and to such, after travail, spring returns. Because Maria Montessori knew both how to impart self-discipline and how to rouse the love of life, she succeeded in ordering the souls of many. Mr. Orem's several books about her imaginative work have done us good service.

Recently a lady author whom I know happened to converse with the editor of the juvenile department of a big New York publishing firm. My friend inquired what sort of books this firm was turning out for children—fantasies, adventure yarns, lively verse? No, nothing like that, the female editor informed her. "We give them new books about love, sex, abortion, and subjects like that—things the modern child is interested in."

That mode of publishing seems an efficient way of producing neurotic children and, eventually, neurotic or psychotic adults. For an early obsession with personal and social "problems" of this character does not result in precocious wisdom: It produces, at best, only an abstract precocious world-weariness—which is quite different from wisdom.

The world of the child rightfully is a world of wonder. If that yearning for the wondrous is denied in childhood, that lack will be manifest later in life. At best, that deficiency will produce a dull adult, easily bored; or, worse, it may lead the young adult to seek a substitute for the legitimate realm of fancy—to seek that substitute in the narcotic trance, for instance, or in obsessive sexuality, or in the kind of fanatic political fantasy we call ideology.

Through creation and fantasy the mind of the child is led to apprehend reality. Allegories, parables, myths, legends, and tales of marvels are not silly; rather, they enable the little boy or girl to grasp certain truths about the human condition, without the painful and sometimes ruinous direct experience of human error. (Indeed, even the wisest and most experienced of us can apprehend ultimate truths only through symbols.) The parables of Hans Christian Andersen, say, are no more false than the parables of Jesus of Nazareth are false.

Pinocchio now is my little daughters' favorite book. They understand the moral aphorisms of the Talking Cricket; they grasp the consequences of the Puppet's misbehavior; they come to perceive in the Fox and the Cat the power of malice in this world. They take a dreadful joy in the perils of their hero, and a quick pleasure in his redemption. With childish intuition, they apprehend something of order in the soul and of temptation in the world. And that sort of learning is pleasurable.

Would it be better for these little girls to be reared on the dreary real-life doings of Dick, Jane, and their dog Spot, in real-life suburbia? Nay, not so: That would only convince them that the realm of literature is a dominion of dullness. Or would it be better for them to develop an infantile "social consciousness" expressed in slogan or cliché, long before they are full members of society? Why, that would be a course of study calculated to develop the priggish busybody. Give the child wonder, and much in creation will remain wonderful always.

Similarly, give direction and discipline and purpose to the child's creative impulses, and the child becomes a genuine human being quite soon, for man is distinguished from brute by his power of orderly creation. Tutor the reason and the senses, and the child will come to serve the divine and the human. But thrust mere abstractions upon the little boy or girl—even if those abstractions are meant to produce the "informed citizen"—and mind and conscience must lie dormant.

Knowing these truths, Maria Montessori skillfully developed means for waking imagination and creative talent that have blossomed for six decades. If every child could be touched by her spirit and her techniques, we would make speedy headway against our present discontents.

Introduction
MONTESSORI: A STRATEGY FOR EDUCATIONAL RENEWAL IN THE 1970s
by Virgil Burns

Legacy and Challenge

WHEN Dr. Maria Montessori opened her first Children's House in a Rome tenement more than sixty years ago, she already had some idea, from her experience with retarded and disturbed children, how her young charges might benefit. What she could not know was the sort of world these children were to inherit. Had more of the world's children been able to attend her schools at the time, the events of the next six decades might not have been so horrendous.

As it has turned out, the world faced by the children of today is filled with even more unpleasant prospects. The legacy they are being left could at best be described as "mixed." The challenges they confront are awesome. That many of them now on the verge of adulthood are bitter about this circumstance is abundantly clear from recent headlines.

They must somehow reduce the destructiveness of mankind and cool his hatreds. They must do this at a time when mankind has at its disposal weapons capable of total annihilation. They must meet the threat to our environment from the noxious products of our not-completely-beneficent technology. They must cope with an explosively expanding population in an era when existing political and economic systems are unable to provide the necessities of life for many, if not most, of the newborn.

13

The Need

If a new generation is to meet these challenges, it must come to the task better equipped than were previous generations. An all-important part of their preparation must be superior education. And what we will state flatly now is simply this:

American education, particularly at the elementary and secondary levels, is not adequate to the job.

Even in the best schools, a small number of our children are condemned to failure. A larger number are doomed to mediocrity. In our worst schools in the great urban ghettos, most of the children are condemned to failure.

This need not be.

The Costs of Failure

The costs of failure are enormous.

For the individual, adequate education can mean the difference between a productive, meaningful life filled with hope or a life of frustration, rejection and despair.

For the affluent, the success of early education is not always a direct prerequisite for future success and happiness. Money can be a great compensator. For those who have money, there is always the possibility of a second chance.

For the poor, however, education, and particularly early education, is crucial. For them there may be no second chance. Once damage has been done, it cannot be undone except at enormous cost to society.

For society in general, the cost of educational failure is almost too high to bear. We are now witnessing the results of a large educationally and economically deprived minority living in the wealthiest society ever known; a minority that is continuously bombarded with advertising for products and a kind of life it has no hope of buying. Who can question the eventual cost of the destruction caused by their circumstances?

But more is needed than simply the prevention of destruction. If our society is to meet successfully the challenges it faces, it cannot afford to waste the potential talents of those of its members now living in deprivation.

These human resources must be conserved. These people must be allowed to become productive.

The principles of education embodied in the Montessori approach can show the way.

The Vision

Dr. Montessori spoke of the power of the child ultimately to regenerate humanity and transform the environment. She called this potential the "secret of childhood." She envisioned a future of universal brotherhood, when man's mission would be to know, love, and serve.

She developed a process of education that is attuned to the child's inner drives, that promotes the beneficial interaction of the child and his surroundings, and that leads to the child's mastery of himself and his environment.

She believed, and it has been proved, that this process can develop children who are confident, competent, self-disciplined, spiritually strong, and, thus, able to work cooperatively for the benefit of society. She believed that such children would lead directly to the creation of a better world. We, who share her vision, believe that its realization is more vital today than ever before.

Self-Motivation

Recent research suggests that how much and how well a person learns throughout his life is determined in large measure by the variety of beneficial experiences he is exposed to during the first years of life.

Dr. Montessori recognized that a child begins learning the moment he enters the world. She was awed by the strength of the child's innate urge to learn. In creating her Children's Houses, she endeavored to establish an environment in which this vital urge would be nurtured and protected.

The environment and the educational materials she created had controls built into them to eliminate obstacles, to encourage beneficial activities, and to correct the child's errors as he worked. Within this controlled environment the child was given the freedom to select his work and to learn at his own pace.

Dr. Montessori found that, as a result, children as young as two and one-half or three were able to work for long periods of time with a great deal of pleasure and little fatigue.

The Approach: Auto-Education

The Montessori approach aims to insure the normal development of the whole personality of the child, of his physical and emotional faculties as well as his intellectual powers. Because the tasks available to the child in a Montessori class are graduated from the simple to the complex and he is free to select his own work and proceed at his own pace, his failures are only temporary and are soon overcome. By learning in this way, the child gains the self-confidence so necessary in the creation of competence.

The large and colorful assortment of scientifically designed materials available to the child enable him to learn by doing. Thus, he is able to get a picture of reality in the concrete before he proceeds to the abstract. Early tasks teach hand-eye coordination, small-muscle control, and relationships in shape and size, color and texture.

The child also learns how to do practical, everyday jobs: how to lace and polish a shoe; how to pour water without spilling a drop; how to serve at table; how to clean up and return things to their proper places.

Also, there are physical exercises to aid in gross as well as refined motor development.

The role of the teacher is to show the child the proper way to use the materials and do the work. The child then teaches himself through his own activity.

Rather than the children's attention being focused collectively on the teacher, the teacher directs her attention primarily to the individual child. Group teaching is not neglected. But when it is used it involves children within the class who happen to have reached, by working at their own pace, similar levels of understanding and are engaged in similar projects.

The directress also maintains discipline. Her aim is not to impose her will on the child but rather to help create a climate of order in which the child can work without interference at meaningful tasks that interest him.

As a result, the child achieves self-discipline. He does so because his activities and his education are directed by his own interest in them and not by pressure from his superiors or by traditional rewards and punishments. His motivations become the adventure of discovery and the joy of accomplishment.

A New Direction

Although the Montessori approach does not provide all the answers to the problems of education that confront us, it does chart a new and superior course in solving them. Furthermore, it is open to the findings of recent research and the introduction of new educational apparatus.

One of its great strengths is its wide application. In addition to enriching the educational experience and insuring the scholastic success of healthy middle-class children, it has been and is being used successfully with children suffering many varieties of handicaps: mental retardation, brain damage, emotional disturbance, blindness, deafness, physical disabilities, and cultural and economic deprivation.

Preface

THE BOOK contains four major sections, in addition to introductory material and appendices. In the first section, brief answers are given to approximately two hundred questions about Montessori, organized under sixty-three topics. This section has grown out of the editor's experiences during more than a decade of researching, writing, and lecturing on Montessori matters. Although the range of topics is not from A to Z, it does cover A to W. A compendium of such scope has not been available heretofore.

In the Introduction to the book, noted Montessorian Virgil Burns offers Montessori as a "strategy" for educational renewal in the 1970s. In the second section, Montessori "tactics" as employed in a variety of Montessori schools are described. It is seen that Montessori schools and programs specify the full self-development of each child as their basic goal. The staff "prepare" the environment with the various Montessori ingredients to foster this development, and impressive results are claimed.

In the third section are a half-dozen selections that explore such topics as the home, discipline, flexibility, public education, language arts, and the Right to Read program—each in relation to contributions the Montessori approach has already made or may potentially make.

In the fourth section is a sampling of materials from various Montessori teacher-training courses, to give the reader a glimpse of the scope and specifics of this phase of Montessori.

In the Appendices are a biographical sketch of the remarkable woman Maria Montessori, a summary of the federally funded Home Start program, and a Montessori discussion outline for individuals or groups.

Section I

A COMPENDIUM OF QUESTIONS AND ANSWERS ON MONTESSORI

If houses suitable for children do not exist, then let us build them.''

—Maria Montessori

What is the house we must build for
our children?
The house we must build is us.
Our attitude.
Our knowledge.
Our desire
to understand their growth.
Our desire
to consciously help their growth.
Our love.
The house where our children most
abide
is us.

by Cele Bona, a Montessori mother

FOR more than ten years the editor has lectured and spoken informally on Montessori topics to varied audiences at colleges and universities, professional conferences, Montessori training courses, parent meetings, and public seminars. One of the most enjoyable aspects of this experience has been the lively question-and-answer sessions that typically follow his Montessori presentations.

Also, numerous readers have, over the years, written the editor for additional information concerning various aspects of Montessori.

Certain questions continue to recur: What happens after my child leaves Montessori? Is there no provision for creativity in Montessori? What is "pure" Montessori? What about the Montessori mystique?

The editor has compiled the questions and queries he receives most frequently from listeners and readers, and has organized them alphabetically by topic, with brief answers. In some cases, a direct quotation from the writings of Dr. Maria Montessori is used to provide the answer.

Topics included in this section appear in the following order:

Absorbent Mind

After Montessori . . .

Auto-Education

Casa dei Bambini

Catholicism

Child

Child as Teacher

Concentration

Creativity

Day Care

Didactic Material

Directress

Disadvantaged

Discipline

Education

Effectiveness of Montessori

Enrollment

"Explosion" in Learning

Formative Period

Franchising

Freedom

Ground Rules

Grouping; Class Size;
    Open Classroom

Head Start

History of Montessori

Imagination

Infighting among
    Montessorians

Intellectual Stimulation

Maria Montessori
Modifying Montessori
Montessori Method
Montessori Movement
Montessori Schools
Montessori's Writings
Motivation
Movement in Education
Mystical Element
"New Education"
Normalized Child
Opposition to Montessori
Order
Outdoors
Play
Practical Life Exercises
Practice
Prepared Environment
Programmed Instruction
Public Education and
  Montessori
Reading
Repetition
Research
Sensitive Periods
Sensory Education
Sharing
Social Development
Sources of Information
  on Montessori
Special Education;
  Retarded Children
Structure
Teacher Training
Toys
Traditional Education
Visiting Montessori Schools
Work

ABSORBENT MIND

What is the "absorbent mind"?

Montessori's term for the young child's remarkable natural capacity to absorb learning directly, without formal instruction, as in mastery of his native language. Also the title of one of her most important books.

AFTER MONTESSORI . . .

How do children from Montessori schools adjust to public school classes?

Quite well, generally, and often above average. For more than a decade, thousands of children all over the country have been making a satisfactory adjustment to public (or other) schools after one or more years in Montessori. Ungraded classes and flexible teachers in the receiving school will help smooth the transition. Sometimes an older Montessori child will "skip" a grade when transferred, but obviously each situation must be evaluated individually.

Montessori children who have developed self-reliance and academic skills usually adapt readily to their new school environment, although the author has heard reports of individual problems. But what of the uncounted numbers of bored and rebellious pupils in public schools who didn't come from Montessori schools?

AUTO-EDUCATION

What is auto-education?
Basically, self-teaching by the child through exercises with materials.

What is the aim of auto-education?
According to Montessori:

> The aim is not an external one, that is to say, it is not the object that the child should learn how to place the cylinders, and that he should know how to perform an exercise. The aim is an inner one, namely, that the child train himself to observe; that he be led to make comparisons between objects, to form judgements, to reason and to decide; and it is in the indefinite repetition of this exercise of attention and of intelligence that a real development ensues.

What evidence is there that the child can teach himself?
Says Montessori: "The child has a mind able to absorb knowledge. He has the power to teach himself. A single observation is enough to prove this. The child grows up speaking his parents' tongue, yet to grown-ups the learning of a language is a very great intellectual achievement."

How can young children in Montessori possibly teach themselves?
The Montessori educational materials are designed to be self-correcting. That is, as the child works with them they provide immediate, tangible checks on his performance. Montessori terms this quality of the material "control of error." Says Montessori: "The educative process is based

on the fact that the control of error lies in the material itself, and the child has concrete evidence of it."

CASA DEI BAMBINI

What was the Casa dei Bambini?

Children's House or House of Childhood. The name given to the first school (and various others) employing the Montessori approach. The original, opened by her in 1907 in the San Lorenzo slum district of Rome, was followed by others in Italy and countries around the world for regular and special students.

What was the chief aim of the original Casa dei Bambini?

According to Montessori, the first Children's House was established "to offer, free of charge, to the children of those parents who are obliged to absent themselves for their work, the personal care which the parents are not able to give." It was, in effect, a day care center with a unique program of cognitive development.

How could this care be offered "free of charge"?

The director of the Roman Association for Good Building had engaged Montessori to establish schools for a very practical reason. The Association's San Lorenzo tenement building, which contained hundreds of apartments, had been hastily and poorly constructed during a short-lived boom, and was in need of repair. In attempting to rehabilitate the apartments, the company found that the young children of working parents were destroying the property.

The plan was to gather groups of these children in large rooms, where their activities would be under the all-day supervision of a teacher. The expenses of the schools would be met by the sum that the Association would have otherwise been forced to spend upon repairs.

What were the school hours recommended by Montessori for these children?

Montessori suggested that "for poor children, and especially for the 'Children's Houses' annexed to workingmen's tenements, the school day should be from nine in the morning to five in the evening in winter, and from eight to six in the summer," explaining that "these long hours are necessary if we are to follow a directed line of action which shall be helpful to the growth of the child."

What was the significance of the Children's House?

According to Montessori, the Casa dei Bambini had dual significance: "the social importance which it assumes through its peculiarity of being a school within the house, and its purely pedagogic importance gained through its methods for the education of very young children."

What did Montessori mean when she said, "We have put the school within the home"?

A large room in the tenement building was designated as the school for children living in the surrounding apartments. The teacher lived in an apartment in the same building, and parents—who, in effect, owned the school —were encouraged to work closely with her.

CATHOLICISM

Is Montessori education basically Catholic? Wasn't Montessori Catholic?

Montessori has been described as a "devout" Catholic, and her written work often reflects her religious beliefs. Although a number of Montessori schools in the U. S. are Catholic-oriented to some degree, most are not. In the majority of Montessori schools, there is no training specific to a particular religious denomination.

CHILD

What, according to Montessori, are the stages of psychic development?

Briefly, Montessori speaks of three general stages of psychic development: from birth to six, six to twelve, and twelve to eighteen. Each contains substages. For example, the first period is subdivided thus: birth to three, when the child "takes in" the environment, and three to six, when he organizes this intake. Even the child's first year of life is composed of several stages, each with its corresponding needs.

How interested in knowledge is the child?
Montessori writes that "the child's love of *knowledge* is such that it surpasses every other love."

Montessori often speaks of the "rights of the child." Did she consider a particular right as most basic?
She believes the fundamental right of the child to be that of the fullest opportunity for his "auto-formation" or self-development.

What did Montessori consider to be the greatest obstacle to the child's self-development?
Unenlightened adults.

How does Montessori define "good"?
For her, "good" pedagogically refers to "the psychological states favorable to the child's development, to his health of mind."
By "evil" she means the psychological states devoid of formative influence or actually unfavorable to his development, since they lead merely to "a useless scattering of his forces."

What are "motives of activity"?
Exercises and materials that capture and hold the child's attention, and impel him to activity. Montessori says that "the work of the child's hands demands 'motives of activity' in the form of suitable objectives. We shall then see small children performing actions that demand an impressive effort."

CHILD AS TEACHER

Are adults really the best teachers for children?
Not according to Montessori, who says that "the best teachers for children are children themselves." Further-

more, "little tots like the company of another child much better than that of an adult."

Can small children be effective "teachers"?

"There are many things," says Montessori, "which no teacher can convey to a child of three, but a child of five can do it with the utmost ease. There is between them a natural mental 'osmosis.' "

But if a small child is occupied with "teaching," won't this delay his own progress?

No, says Montessori. "In the first place, he does not teach all the time and his freedom is respected. Secondly, teaching helps him to understand what he knows even better than before. He has to analyze and rearrange his little store of knowledge before he can pass it on."

CONCENTRATION

What inspired Montessori to develop her educational method?

In a talk given before the National Education Association, Montessori related the episode that "made me decide to plan out a special method for the education of children." The incident involved her observation of a child who, with phenomenal concentration, repeatedly performed a task. In Montessori's words:

> I was making the first experiments in San Lorenzo [Rome], trying to apply my principles and part of the material that I had previously used in the education of backward children.

> A little girl, about three years of age, was deeply absorbed in the work of placing wooden blocks and cylinders in a frame for that purpose. The expression of her face was that of such intense attention, that it was almost a revelation to me. Never before had I seen a child look with such "fixedness" upon an object, and my conviction about the instability of attention which goes incessantly from one thing to another, a fact which is so characteristic

in little children, made the phenomenon the more remarkable to me.

I watched the child without interrupting her, and counted how many times she would do her work over and over. It seemed that she was never going to stop. As I saw that it would take a very long time, I took the little armchair on which she was sitting and placed child and chair on the big table. Hastily she put the frame across the chair, gathered blocks and cylinders in her lap, and continued her work undisturbed. I invited the other children to sing, but the little girl went on with her work and continued even after the singing had ceased. I counted forty-four different exercises which she made, and when she finally stopped, and did so absolutely independently from an exterior cause that could disturb her, she looked around with an expression of great satisfaction, as if she were awakening from a deep and restful sleep.

Is the small child really capable of extended concentration?
According to Montessori, "The powers of concentration shown by little children from three to four years old have no counter-part save the annals of genius."

How important did Montessori consider a child's concentration to be?
Montessori refers to concentration as "the center of development," adding that "the first essential for the child's development is concentration. It lays the whole basis for his character and social behavior. He must find out how to concentrate, and for this he needs things to concentrate upon."

CREATIVITY

What place is there in Montessori for the child's creativity? Does Montessori training stifle creativity?
Montessori, while making adequate provision for dramatics, music, drawing, and the like, views creativity with a much broader perspective. She considers the child's total development as creative. With his own power, he creates a

personality—a man. This is his "great work." The Montessori apparatus can be used imaginatively.

Regina Barnett of the Fox Valley Montessori School (Aurora, Ill.) offers a one-week "Montessori Approach to Creative Activities" course to professionals, aides, and parents involved with preschool children. Lectures on the creative process and its development include the work of Dr. Victor Lowenfeld and Rhoda Kellogg. Participants also do about twenty creative activities, each of which involves a physical skill, design, and media such as paint, varieties of paper, and clay. These activities can then, for example, be utilized as a resource in the classroom.

DAY CARE

Is Montessori applicable to day care facilities?
The Montessori method—principles and practices—is being successfully utilized in an ever-increasing number of day care centers and programs.

The Assumption Montessori Training Course (Philadelphia, Pa.), codirected by Miss Marianne Moore, offers an AMI Primary Diploma. In the past few years the Training Course has cooperated with the Philadelphia Board of Education in setting up twelve Montessori classes in Head Start centers or Get-Set day care centers. Teachers for these classes have come principally from the Assumption Montessori Training Center. The Center has been instrumental in the starting of a Montessori class in a public school.

DIDACTIC MATERIAL

What is the didactic material?
Essentially, a systematic array of objects resembling learning games, each of which is carefully designed to impart particular learnings. There are materials of wood,

metal, cardboard, etc., for sensory education, mathematics, language, science, and other areas. The materials are usually manipulatable and contain "control of error" enabling the learner to work alone successfully.

Why is the didactic material so important within the Montessori method?

Montessori summarizes the function of the material in this way:

> Our didactic material renders auto-education possible and permits a methodical education of the senses. Not upon the ability of the teachers does such education rest, but upon the didactic system. This presents objects which, first, attract the spontaneous attention of the child, and second, contain a rational gradation of stimuli.

Since there is no Montessori school close by, could I order the Montessori materials for my child?

This is generally not practical. A complete set of materials costs several thousand dollars. If a parent obtained the material for her child, it would be essential—if they were to serve the specific purposes for which they were designed—that she learn how and when to demonstrate the correct use of the various pieces, which requires considerable training.

Must the didactic material be used in only one way? Is no flexibility or experimentation permitted? I heard an educator say there is too much ritual concerning the use of these materials.

Children discover many ingenious and innovative ways to use the materials. For example, many children trace a metal inset in the prescribed fashion and then proceed to elaborate the geometric design into a complete picture. Writes Montessori:

> If the child uses the material either in accordance with the instructions of the mistress or in some other way invented by himself which shows intelligent modifications, then the teacher will leave the child to go on repeating the same

exercise or making his own attempts and experiments. She will let the child have as much time as he wants without ever interrupting his activity.

But the children are not allowed to abuse the materials.

Why, in the Montessori environment, is the number of each kind of didactic object limited?
Explains Montessori:

There is only one specimen of each object, and if a piece is in use when another child wants it, the latter—if he is "normalized"—will wait for it to be released. Important social qualities derive from this. The child comes to see that he must respect the work of others, not because someone has said he must, but because this is a reality that he meets in his daily experience. There is only one between many children, so there is nothing for it but to wait. And since this happens every hour of the day for years, the idea of respecting others, and of waiting one's turn, becomes an habitual part of life which always grows more mature.

Where can the didactic material be obtained?
Some is manufactured in the U. S. Much of it is imported from Holland. Some Montessorians make many items themselves. Certain distributors will sell the materials only to registered Montessori schools or teachers.
For information:

Montessori Leermiddelenhuis
A. Nienhuis N.V.
14 Industriepark
Zelhem (Gld.), Holland

C. Baroni and G. Manangon
46023 Gonzaga
Mantova, Italy

Were not the Montessori materials developed with retarded

or *"deficient" children? Are such materials appropriate for "normal" children?*

The materials were derived from experiments of Montessori and others who worked with "deficient," "culturally disadvantaged," "normal," and other categories of children. She was greatly influenced by the work of Itard and Seguin, two pioneers in what has come to be known as "special education." (All three were medical doctors.)

DIRECTRESS

Why is the Montessori teacher often referred to as a "directress"?

For the traditional teacher, Montessori substituted the "didactic material" which, by containing "control of error" makes "auto-education" practical. Says Montessori: "The teacher has thus become a *director* of the spontaneous work of the children."

Montessori generally employs the feminine "directress," although it is interesting to note that an increasing number of men are joining the ranks of Montessori teachers and administrators.

The Montessori method has been described as a "method of nonintervention." Does this mean that the directress should never intervene directly?

Montessori says that "the educator must, to the greatest possible extent, limit his intervention," but she makes it quite clear that the directress should intervene when necessary:

> Non-intervention is only appropriate when some interesting phenomenon is taking place in the child's life; it is quite out of place when disorder reigns and the attention of the child is all astray. . . . The directress should not only intervene when there is disorder, but also beforehand to prevent it coming.

According to Montessori, "in the quality of this

intervention lies the art which makes up the individuality of the teachers."

Why are Montessori teachers in American schools frequently from other countries?

The limited supply of American-born Montessori teachers has necessitated "importing" Montessori teachers from Ceylon, Holland, England, and numerous other countries. The Montessori teacher supply-and-demand situation is improving as teacher-training programs expand in the U. S.

How and where does one hire Montessori teachers?

Demand for good Montessori teachers nationally continues to exceed the supply. Schools in need of teachers recruit by various methods: advertising in newspapers, Montessori newsletters, periodicals; word of mouth, at conferences, etc.; contacting Montessori training courses, teacher associations, and other organizations. *Children's House* magazine (P.O. Box 111, Caldwell, N. J. 07006) regularly publishes Montessori "teacher wanted" and "position wanted" ads.

Children's House is a useful publication for the parent or professional interested in Montessori matters. The following is excerpted from a review of *Children's House* which appeared in *Library Journal* (a Bowker/ Xerox publication, 1974):

> Primarily the voice for the Montessori educator. Each 40-page issue includes three to four articles on new methods in teaching, and more particularly techniques of reaching out for alternative ways of educating children both in the classroom and at home. Articles are by teachers and laymen. They are well written, lively and often controversial. Departments include reviews of records and films, and books—primarily for children, rather than about children. The reviews are first rate, give an added dimension to other traditional journals in the field. Which is to say the reader does not have to be an advocate of the Montessori method to profit from this nicely edited magazine.

How can one directress possibly control the behavior of

twenty or more children who are in different parts of a room or even in several rooms?

Unlike many traditional teachers, the directress normally does not have to control behavior directly. Rather, the interesting didactic materials and exercises channel each child's interests and energies along constructive lines.

Says Montessori, "When the child educates himself, and when the control and correction of errors is yielded to the didactic material, there remains for the teacher nothing but to observe."

What are the functions of the Montessori directress?

Preparing the environment and maintaining it with the help of the children; observing the children; providing a model for the children (in the quality of her speech, for example); demonstrating materials and exercises; matching appropriate materials with individual needs. Two of her main duties could be summarized as (1) learning from the child, and (2) serving the child's development indirectly.

What is the basic difference between the role of the Montessori directress and that of the traditional teacher?

The directress prepares the environment for auto-education, then observes as the children teach themselves individually with special materials; the traditional teacher is typically an "authority" who dispenses information to a seated group. Thus, the Montessori learning situation features a directress observing individuals manipulating materials, while traditional education usually involves an adult teaching a class.

Put another way, the work of the directress consists of "protecting the child's creative powers and directing them without disturbing them in their expansion."

Does the directress ever "teach"?

She gives individual and group lessons as needed. Many schools employ specialists in, say, foreign language or music, to give instruction at specified times.

According to Montessori, what are the characteristics of a good lesson?

"Brevity, simplicity, and objectivity."

According to Montessori, what is the fundamental quality of a directress?

Her "capacity for observation," which must be coupled with "the desire to observe." Furthermore: "On this observation of minute details depends the order or the disorder of the children; on it depends the results she will obtain in her school."

Two of the most fundamental characteristics could be labeled as "skill" and "spirit": *Skill*—in observation, knowledge of materials, etc.; *Spirit*—dedication, patience, etc.

For a detailed discussion of the importance of the directress's personality, training, and experience, see *The Children's House Parent-Teacher Guide to Montessori,* edited by Ken Edelson and R. C. Orem.

How does one acquire the necessary skill in observation?

Says Montessori, "Actual training and practice are necessary to fit for this method teachers who have not been prepared for scientific observation."

Do Montessori schools use teacher aides or so-called paraprofessionals to assist the directress?

Many do.

The Deerfield Montessori School (Deerfield, Ill.) sponsors a "Work/Study Program for Assistant Teachers," in conjunction with the work/study program of the Deerfield High School. For example, a high school senior girl will work as an assistant teacher five afternoons per week for the full school year under the supervision of the directress, and will be paid as a regular staff member.

A second program is for college students in the "Independent Study Program." For them, Deerfield Montessori School offers a condensed version of the year-long program. The college students, from such schools as DePauw University and Lake Forest College, work five half-days per week for one month as volunteer assistant teachers. In addition, they do a research paper.

According to Deerfield Montessori School directors
Carolyn Kambich and Theresa Fine:

> We find the high school and college students who come
> to our schools quite refreshing as they seem to intuitively
> grasp the wonder of the "normalized child." They look at
> the children in the mini-society of the classroom and
> simply comment, "How beautiful these children are"—
> quite a contrast to some of the more sophisticated adults
> investigating pre-school programs who would like to know
> "at what age the children begin reading, etc."
> In general, we find that those who would really begin to
> comprehend the depths of the Montessori philosophy
> must do as the researcher Maria Montessori did—go to the
> primary source—the children.

DISADVANTAGED

*Does the Montessori method work with so-called culturally
disadvantaged children?*

The Montessori "prepared environment" approach is
being employed with considerable success in the increasing
number of programs for various "disadvantaged" popula-
tions, such as inner-city Negro children.

DISCIPLINE

What is Montessori's view of discipline?

Montessori speaks of the truly disciplined child as
achieving inner discipline through activity. Allowed to
choose interesting work, to become absorbed in it, and to
complete it, he develops concentration, habits of order and
work, and self-discipline.

*Don't Montessori teachers ever have "discipline prob-
lems"?*

Yes. Although the Montessori environment can exert a
therapeutic effect, it is worth noting that one Montesori-
an—a psychiatrist—believes on the basis of screening he

has done that approximately one in five applicants for Montessori schooling needs some type of outside help before he can benefit fully from the "prepared environment."

How does a Montessori teacher handle a problem child?

There are many possible courses of action, only a few of which can be suggested here. Depending upon the child and circumstances, she might direct his energy toward the didactic material or a "practical life exercise." If necessary, the child will be shunted away from his peers temporarily. Perhaps the directress will decide to confer with the parents. Many schools utilize professional consultant or referral resources. In extreme cases, the parents will be asked to withdraw a child who is too disturbed or disruptive.

EDUCATION

How did Montessori define "education"?

According to Montessori, education consists of the "active help given to the normal expansion of the life of the child."

When should education begin?

According to Montessori, education should begin "at birth."

What, according to Montessori, characterizes an educator?

Says Montessori, "The educator must be as one inspired by a deep *worship of life,* and must, through this reverence, *respect,* while he observes with human interest, the *development* of the child life."

What did Montessori consider the true aim of education?

Above all, *to help life.* Also, to aid human development by discovering and liberating the child.

EFFECTIVENESS OF MONTESSORI

Is the Montessori movement just another educational fad? Is Montessori here to stay?

Much recent research in the behavioral sciences supports the basic principles underlying the Montessori method, and the number of Montessori schools in the United States alone has grown from one in 1958 to over 1,500 in the 1970s.

There is considerable reason to believe that the Montessori approach will continue to gain in support and implementation, but its ultimate impact, of course, remains to be seen.

Montessori sounds good in theory. Does it really work?

The rapid spread of new Montessori schools in the U. S. during the past decade, often in the face of determined opposition from the educational establishment, is some indication of parental satisfaction with the results of the method. The limited research available on the effectiveness of the Montessori method is favorable. Of course, Montessori schools have thrived in many other countries, such as Holland, for decades.

I don't believe the Montessori method or any other approach is the "cure-all" for "problem children."

Montessori didn't claim her method was successful with all such children. For example, one of the rules of the first Children's House was that "those children who show themselves to be incorrigible shall be expelled from the 'Children's House.'"

ENROLLMENT

I have a five-year-old and the local Montessori school won't take him.

Many Montessori directresses will not accept such "older" children—unless they have prior Montessori training. By age five, certain "sensitive periods" are past, and the program may be less suited to the child. Also, schools naturally give preference to younger children who will likely be in the program for several years.

At what age should a child start in a Montessori school?

Many directresses say the ideal age is between two and one-half and three and one-half. Many children start later however, and Montessori day care centers are enrolling some children at an earlier age.

Good results can be obtained with children who enter between the ages of three and one-half and four and one-half, especially if they remain in the school for a three-year cycle of Montessori learning.

When during the school year can a child enroll in a Montessori school?

Ordinarily, at any time there is a vacancy. Since each child begins work with the material at a level suited for him and progresses at his own individual learning rate, there is little concern with his being "behind" (or "ahead") of the other children. He is guided by his own interests, rhythm, and capacities.

Do Montessori schools provide transportation?

The majority do not. Parents often form car pools.

I have the impression that Montessori is expensive. What is the tuition at Montessori schools?

It varies greatly depending upon the particular school, whether the child attends a half-day or full-day session, etc. The typical range is $400 to $800 per year per child, but tuition can exceed $1,000 per year, and one subsidized Montessori program for poor children charges parents $2.00 per year.

Would it be better to invest in Montessori for my child now or save for his college education?

A Montessori education during his early formative years can help your child develop desirable attitudes, habits, and competencies of lasting benefit. Money spent during this period can have a much greater effect in guiding his development than later expenditures.

Are scholarships or other financial aid available?

Many Montessori schools offer a limited number of full or partial scholarships.

"EXPLOSION" IN LEARNING

What does Montessori mean by "explosion" in learning?

Prolonged involvement by the child in one type of work exclusively, lasting as long as several days (a phenomenon which, incidentally, "explodes" the popular notion of an inherently short attention span in young children). As Montessori explains:

> The directress should not, however, become alarmed if the children give themselves up exclusively for several days to one kind of work: this is what we call an "explosion"; and this continuous application to one kind of work—provided it is done with intensity, that is to say, with sincerity—always produces the best results.

What is an example of such an "explosion"?
One of the best known is the "explosion into writing," which Montessori discusses:

> Children who are able to commence writing at the proper age (i.e., four-and-a-half or five years of age) reach a perfection in writing which you will not find in children who have begun to write at six or seven; but especially you will not find in this later stage that richness of production, which has made us call this singular phenomenon "the explosion into writing."

FORMATIVE PERIOD

Why are the first six years of life so important?
They constitute what Montessori terms the "formative period," the crucial time when the child's fundamental patterns of personality are developed.

FRANCHISING

I recently saw the newspaper ad of a Montessori franchise outfit.
Several firms are involved in marketing Montessori or other early-childhood-education approaches, with varying results. How successful such efforts will be on a large scale and over a period of time remains to be seen. One very real problem is that of maintaining quality control.

FREEDOM

Is it true that children in Montessori have too much freedom?
Won't too much freedom lead to chaos? Are there any rules the Montessori children must follow?

Children in the "prepared environment" are free to make many decisions, but the "organization of work" coupled with a limited number of "ground rules" provides sufficient order. In sum, the Montessori setting offers "liberty within limits," not license to do anything one pleases.

GROUND RULES

What are the Montessori "ground rules"?

As the term implies, they establish certain limits enabling even a large number of children to move and work in close proximity harmoniously. For example, one ground rule states that a child may not interfere with another child or his work. But he is allowed to join him in an activity if invited by that child to do so.

What are some other ground rules?

In the Children's House, the child can move about quite freely, but not run or push. He can talk softly, whenever the need arises, but not shout. When he is finished working with a piece of material, he must return it in proper condition to its particular place, ready for the next user.

The AMS-affiliated New World School (Hackensack and Paramus, N. J.) has developed the following chart which depicts concisely the child's rights and responsibilities in the Montessori classroom setting.

Jo Wood Savoye, founder and owner of the New World School, is a leading Montessorian who has taught at Campus-Free College (Boston, Mass.) and Leonia Free School (Leonia, N. J.).

CHILD'S RIGHTS

The child is free to work with any material displayed in the environment.

The child may work on a table or a rug, whichever is suitable to the work chosen.

The child has the freedom to use the room as his needs dictate in the above rights.

The child has the right to work undistracted by others. He may initiate, complete, or repeat an exercise alone and without a break in his concentration cycle.

CHILD'S RESPONSIBILITIES

He must use it respectfully; that is, he must not harm the material, himself, or others. He may not use it in a way that disturbs the activities of others in the environment.

He may not work at, or on, a display shelf as his presence there would obstruct the other children's access to the materials.

The child restores the environment during and after an exercise. He is responsible for mopping his own spills, rolling his own rug, placing his chair under his spot at the table, and returning his work to the appropriate spot on the shelf.

No child touches the work of another without his invitation to do so. No child is allowed to interfere with another's learning cycle. (This provides security for the child involved in an exercise to continue it to its completion.) If he must leave his work temporarily,

The child has a right not to join a group activity. He may continue working with the individual exercises during group activities, or he may stand apart as an observer of group activities without becoming an active participant.

He can continue later, confident that it will be as he left it when he returns.

He is not allowed to interfere or disrupt an activity he has chosen not to join; this is his responsibility to the group.

The child has a right to work alone.

A child is not forced or even encouraged to share work. Generosity develops from within as a child matures and gains self-security. With adequate materials and supportive ground rules, sharing comes naturally, in cases where sharing is appropriate or necessary.

The child has a right to do nothing if he desires. He may be learning by observing others; he may be thinking; or he may simply be relaxing.

His idleness is not allowed to disturb or distract others' activities.

GROUPING; CLASS SIZE; OPEN CLASSROOM

How many grades are there in a Montessori school?

Classes in a Montessori school are typically ungraded—organized by age groupings rather than by traditional compartmentalized grades. For example, the "beginner" class will have three-, four-, and five-year-olds; the next class will have six-, seven-, and eight-year-olds. Interestingly, the concept of the ungraded or nongraded class has come into educational vogue in recent years. Montessori was practicing it over sixty years ago.

In their useful brochure "A Close Look at the Montessori Primary Classroom," staff of the Montessori Schools of Omaha (Mrs. Mary Verschuur, head directress) discuss open classrooms and free schools in relation to the Montessori primary class. For this inexpensive publication and other titles, the reader should contact Montessori Schools of Omaha, P.O. Box 6252, Omaha, Neb. 68106.

One example of training for adults offered by the Children's Center (Tenafly, N. J.) is the Open Classroom Workshop, sponsored by the National Association of Independent Schools. The aim of this workshop is to provide teachers with the opportunity to learn about the underlying principles and operating procedures that facilitate the conduct of open classrooms. A workshop format is used so that teachers can learn from children, from the workshop staff, from the environment and from one another. Participants have the oppportunity to explore:
   —classroom arrangement and management
   —equipment needed (manufactured and impro-
   vised)
   —the rationale of a "living and doing" school
   program
   —the importance of modern psychological contributions
   —development of reading, language, and math
   skills
   —curriculum implications in math, language arts,
   movement and music, science, art
   —group dynamics
   — systems of record keeping for the teacher and
   the child in an "open environment."

The workshop is directed by Mrs. Suzanne M.

Spector, director of The Children's Center, and Miss Valerie Jameson, experienced British infant school teacher from Leicestershire, England.

Why have a three-year age range in one class?
A child can learn with older children in one subject, younger children in another, and children his own age in a third. The three-year age range allows for much greater flexibility of programming and meeting of individual needs. Freed of the traditional grouping by grades, students in the ungraded class can work at whatever level is appropriate. The younger children learn from observing the older, who can also help teach them directly.

Doesn't "individualized education" require that classes be kept quite small?
No. Since children with the didactic equipment in a Montessori environment spend most of their time teaching themselves or each other, the teacher is freed to give lessons to individuals or small groups as needed.

One usually associates Montessori with the preschool years. Is Montessori applicable to the elementary grades and above?
Although the Montessori approach is still most widely employed with three-, four-, and five-year-olds, an increasing number of schools are instituting junior classes enabling children from six to nine years of age, and even older, to continue in Montessori. A few Montessori schools in this country (and many abroad) have Montessori through the twelfth grade.

Thus, the value of Montessori is not confined to programs for younger children. Her educational principles are applicable to the learning process from "pre-nursery through post-university."

There is much emphasis in education these days upon lowering the teacher/pupil ratio through reduction of class size, yet Montessori classes are often relatively large.
Many Montessori teachers consider a class of about twenty-five children the ideal size. There should be enough children in each age group to form a balanced population

and allow sufficient diversity for children to learn from each other.

Teacher/pupil ratios must be discussed in relation to the age range of the students and the format of the learning environment. A traditionally taught class of twenty seated children all close in age offers less opportunity for truly individualized education than a Montessori class of twenty-five children with a three-year age range working alone or in small groups as the directress observes and moves about giving individual lessons. And the author has seen some Montessori classes of thirty-five or more students functioning effectively.

Was Montessori interested in the child below age three?

Montessori became increasingly interested in the application of her principles to child-rearing from birth to age three. She spoke of the need for a "science of child-rearing," and for "education from the moment of birth."

HEAD START

Has Head Start utilized Montessori?

To a disappointingly small degree. Only a relative handful of Head Start projects have utilized Montessori. Yet, Head Start projects have often lacked adequate structure and direction, and objective evaluation of Head Start to date has not been especially favorable.

HISTORY OF MONTESSORI

Why didn't the Montessori method "take" the first time it was introduced in America, prior to World War I?

There were undoubtedly many contributing causes, of varying significance, including hostility of a defensive educational establishment; lack of effective organization and management within the movement; "infighting" and divisiveness among Montessorians; overcommercialization of didactic materials; failure to institutionalize teacher training; Montessori principles too dissonant with the psychology then in vogue, and so on.

Who is Nancy Rambusch?

Milwaukee-born Mrs. Nancy McCormick Rambusch took Montessori training in London in 1953, taught Montessori in New York City, then helped found (1958) and direct Whitby School (Greenwich, Conn.), the first of the new Montessori schools in America. Described in *Newsweek* as the "red-haired dynamo of the Montessori revival," she was a founder of the American Montessori Society (1960). Her book, *Learning How to Learn,* was published in 1962. (Incidentally, a biographical guide identifying the achievements of past and present leaders in Montessori is needed.)

IMAGINATION

I've heard that Montessori does not provide the child sufficient opportunity to develop and use his imagination.

Montessori believes that the very young child's imagination can best be served by sensory education and training in observation. According to her, imagination is developed from reality-impressions received from the environment, thus the need for training in perceiving the environment.

INFIGHTING AMONG MONTESSORIANS

Montessorians seem to fight a great deal among themselves.

Some would-be Montessorians waste valuable time and energy—and create considerable confusion—by engaging in what one observer has aptly summarized as "low-budget politics."

The Montessori movement, so-called, has its share of personality clashes, power struggles and petty bickering so characteristic of popular movements.

An article, "Montessori: Madness Over the Method," in a national news magazine alluded to this infighting.

> The Montessori method was developed seven decades ago to teach retarded children in Rome, but now it is rapidly winning over thousands of affluent American parents who are eager to give their pre-school children a

This

head start in learning. Today, there are some 1,300 Montessori schools in the U. S., with tuitions ranging from $400 to $1,600 annually, and new ones are opening at the rate of 75 a year. But even as Montessori booms in the U. S., its adherents are engaged in a bitter struggle to determine who are the "real" Montessorians. [*Newsweek*, Nov. 20, 1972]

Doesn't this divisiveness among Montessorians hurt their cause?

Surely. Montessorians must present a reasonably united front if they are to gain public and professional support.

INTELLECTUAL STIMULATION

Aren't we "robbing children of childhood" with such programs as Montessori? Shouldn't childhood be reserved for "fun things"? There is plenty of time later for school.

Children, of course, are in school—Montessori or otherwise—for only part of the day. They have opportunity after school, on weekends, during vacations, etc., for nonschool activities.

Children are eager to learn. They will never be more ready. Montessori helps them learn *how* to learn. According to Benjamin Bloom, 50 percent of the child's intelligence is formed by age four. Montessori provides a prepared environment to tap the potential of the young learner's absorbent mind and sensitive periods for sensory, motor, and intellectual education.

Erik Erikson refers to the child's "sense of industry" and his "pleasure of work completion," which is developed by "steady attention and persevering diligence."

Dr. Montessori recognized that the very young child goes through periods of great sensitivity in particular areas, during which he learns more easily than at any other time in his life.

The first six years are the child's most critical years of development. The very young child possesses an unusual sensitivity and capacity to absorb and learn from his environment.

Don't most children already get enough intellectual stimulation at home, without Montessori?

Such stimulation varies tremendously in quantity and quality with each child's situation, and is usually not carefully planned or presented. The Montessori didactic material in the prepared environment offers the child a measured exposure; he can select tasks appropriate for himself and progress at his own rate. The Montessori method provides for the child's balanced physical, emotional, intellectual, and social development.

Each child is given the opportunity to enhance his visual, aural, tactile, and kinesthetic skills. The carefully organized sequence of materials graduated in difficulty enables him to develop clear concepts of weight, texture, size, shape, color, and so on.

MARIA MONTESSORI

Was Montessori a medical doctor?

Yes. At age twenty-six, she received a "double honors" degree as Doctor of Medicine and Surgery at the University of Rome (the first woman to complete medical training in Italy). She was assistant doctor at the University Psychiatric Clinic, Director of the Medical Pedagogical Institute, and also a private physician.

How did Montessori become interested in the education of children?

While assistant doctor at the Psychiatric Clinic of the University of Rome, her attention was caught by the plight of the "idiot children" who at that time were housed in general insane asylums with adults. She studied the special educational methods devised for such children by Edouard Seguin (another physician-educator). Gradually she became convinced that mental deficiency presented more a *pedagogical* than a *medical* problem. She began to teach "feebleminded" children and to train teachers for such children, as her interest in education deepened.

What were some of her other accomplishments?

Montessori was a skilled educational researcher; prolific

author; innovator of didactic equipment and children's furniture; gifted lecturer; and world traveler.

Why did Montessori decide to apply her method to normal children?

Using her method, Montessori was able to teach a number of deficient children from the Rome asylums to read and write well enough to pass the public school examination. She believed the deficients succeeded because they had been taught differently. Their development had been aided, while the normal children had been held back by traditional education.

She decided to apply her method experimentally to normal children, convinced that it would "set free or develop their personalities in a marvelous and surprising way."

Did Montessori ever visit the United States?

Twice. She came in late 1913 for a lecture tour, and again in 1915 to give a summer course at the Panama-Pacific Exposition, which was held to celebrate the completion of the Panama Canal.

MODIFYING MONTESSORI

Do you believe any of the Montessori method should be modified?

Her methods and materials can and should be supplemented and elaborated within our current understanding of learning theory; the educational technology now available could revolutionize the application of her approach, which should be teamed with the "systems approach" to education, programmed learning, computer-assisted instruction, and other electronic developments.

Dr. Ann Lucas, Professor of Psychology at Fairleigh Dickinson University (Teaneck, N. J.) and director of the Montessori training program there, describes it as the "oldest ongoing Montessori program in the country, having started in 1964."

Twelve graduate credits, which may be applied

toward an M.A. in child development, are given. According to Dr. Lucas, "in grounding students in Montessori education, we also try to escape the 'mystique' of uncritical acceptance of all that Montessori recommended. We attempt to broaden the perspective of students by exposing them to the wider literature of psychology and education."

MONTESSORI METHOD

What is the Montessori method?
An educational approach that frees the child's potential for self-development and offers the external means necessary for this development. A three-part (motor, sensory, intellectual) sequence of materials and activities enables the child to teach himself in a prepared environment under the observation of a specially trained "directress."

According to Montessori, what is the fundamental principle of her method?
"The *liberty of the pupil,* permitting a development of individual, spontaneous manifestations of the child's nature."

The Montessori method is a "foreign" system developed for Italian children at the turn of the century, is it not?
The Montessori method has continued to evolve in scores of countries around the world since she opened her first Children's House in 1907.

What is the most significant effect of the Montessori method upon children?
Declares Montessori:

> We find this phenomenon—the establishment of normality* in children—repeated unfailingly in all our schools, with children belonging to different social classes, races, and cultures. It is the single most important result of our whole work.

*See the topic Normalized Child in this section.

Was the Montessori method original with Dr. Montessori?

In developing the method that bears her name, Montessori drew upon various sources: the work of other educators (Itard, Seguin, etc.); her teachers (Anna Maccheroni, etc.); observation of her own pupils. In *The Montessori Method,* she freely acknowledges the eclectic origins of her approach, and says, "Thus, my ten years of work may in a sense be considered as a summing up of the forty years of work done by Itard and Seguin."

Who was Itard?

Jean Itard (1775–1838), student of Pinel, was a French physician-educator who worked with deaf-mutes and spent years attempting to educate the feral "wild boy" of Aveyron. Itard is quoted at length by Montessori.

According to Montessori, what was really responsible for the spread of her method?

Says Montessori: "It is the children themselves who spread my method. Happily, they behave as I say they do in my books, and people go and see them, and at last believe in it themselves."

MONTESSORI MOVEMENT

What is the extent of the Montessori movement in the United States?

As a movement, Montessori is still relatively small, loosely organized, and limited in influence. The American Montessori Society provides some direction nationally. The Association Montessori Internationale claims a more international orientation. Only a fraction of one percent of our annual educational expenditure in this country is for support of Montessori activities.

How extensive is Montessori teacher training in America?

Until recently there have been but a handful of training courses in the entire country, training a total of only several hundred teachers annually. Several universities have initiated Montessori teacher training and other institutions of higher learning can be expected to follow suit. We may see a considerable expansion of Montessori teacher training as business firms move into this field.

How many Montessori schools are there in the United States?

There are more than 1,500 schools employing the Montessori approach, with the number continuing to increase at the rate of 75 to 100 each year. They range from new schools of fewer than 20 children to well-established ones enrolling 200 or more children. There are clusters of Montessori schools in such areas as metropolitan Washington, D.C., Chicago, New York City, St. Paul–Minneapolis, etc.

The Illinois Montessori Society conducts a comprehensive annual survey of Montessori programs in Illinois and adjacent locations. Here are some of the more important findings of the latest survey as reported by the Society:

Sixty-two Montessori schools, centers and children's houses—serving the child in Illinois and four adjacent locations—have 5,059 children enrolled in pre-schools, toddler (2-year-old) groups, and elementary classes as of December, 1973.

Here are the statistics: Children 3–6 years: 4,385; 2-years: 205; elementary: 469. Day care is provided for 375 of these children.

This is how Montessori in Illinois has grown since the census was begun in 1967:

'67	1,750	'71	3,330
'68	2,200	'72	4,381
'69	2,850	'73	5,059
'70	3,250		

So, as the Society notes, Montessori enrollment in the Illinois area is "5,000+ and growing!"

Four schools serve 200 or more children: *Lisle, Ancona*–Chicago, *Alcuin*–Oak Park. *Near North*–Chicago (each also offers elementary). Serving more than 100 children (but less than 200) are: *Countryside*–Northbrook, *Deerfield,* including its Highland Park center, *South Shore* and its annex–Chicago. *Knox*–Wilmette, *Chiaravalle*–Evanston, *Champaign*–Urbana. *Children's Center of Schaumbert, Beverly*–Chicago, *Seton*–Clarendon Hills, *Park Ridge, Forest Park, Joliet, Rogers Park*–Chicago, *Calumet Region*–Hobart and *Lake Forest.*

Montessori tuition costs, the survey indicates, vary widely:
Pre-school tuition averages $566 per year for a 3-hour session; pre-school tuition ranges from $400–$800.

Four schools are not tabulated: *Earth Child*-Chicago Heights is free, *Chicago Urban Day* and *Ezzard Charles,* a sliding scale and also provide day care, and *Holy Family* charges $100 per year.

Elementary range is $675–$1250 with the average for 11 schools as $937.

Why the interest in Montessori now?
The popularity that the Montessori movement has enjoyed to date has hardly been the result of astute planning or strong organization at the national level. Rather, this popularity can be attributed to such factors as:
   a. the dissatisfaction of parents with other available educational programs, and their search for alternatives.
   b. the compatibility of Montessori principles with recent findings in the behavioral sciences.
   c. considerable favorable publicity, including articles in major magazines and newspapers. (See, for example, "Make Mine Montessori," by Emily Lambert, *Parents' Magazine,* July, 1973.)

When did the renewed American interest in Montessori begin?

This interest can be dated from June, 1953, when an article by Mrs. Nancy Rambusch, "Learning Made Easy," appeared in *Jubilee* magazine. The article, describing certain aspects of the Montessori method, signaled the "rebirth" of Montessori in America.

MONTESSORI SCHOOLS

How can I identify a good Montessori school?

Observe the children at work in the school. Examine the physical plant, furnishings, and equipment. Talk with the staff and ascertain their qualifications (training, experience, etc.). Become familiar with the programs. Talk with parents. Then evaluate what you have found, using the guide in *A Montessori Handbook*, by R. C. Orem. This guide, which discusses the philosophy, physical plant, personnel, program, and pupils in an effective school, was selected by the Illinois Montessori Society for inclusion in its standard information packet. The American Montessori Society also distributes a useful guide, "Basic Characteristics of a Montessori Program for 3 to 6 Year Old Children," which answers the question: What are the salient features to be looked for in a Montessori primary program?

The following listing, by Lillian DeVault, Sonja Donahue, and Jo Savoye, is the most current guide provided by the American Montessori Society.

GROWTH IN THE CHILD

—Independent
—Self-directed
—Responsible group member
—Self-disciplined
—Self-accepting
—Enjoys learning
—A unique individual

THE PROGRAMMED LEARNING ENVIRONMENT
—Full range of sequentially structured developmental aids

—Minimum of 35 square feet per child, over and above space for furnishings
—Light-weight, proportionate, movable child-sized furnishings
—Identifiable ground rules

PROGRAM ORGANIZATION
—Ungraded mix of three-year age span
—Enrollment age between 2.6 and 3.6
—Policy of three-year cycle of attendance
—Five-day week with a minimal daily three-hour session
—Separate, small groups. Specially designed orientation program for new children
—Observational records of the individual child and the classroom life
—Public observation policy

PROGRAM EMPHASIS
—Auto-education
—Real tasks available (as opposed to role playing)
—Intrinsic motivation
—Process, not product
—Cooperation, not competition
—Fostering autonomy in the child
—Fostering competencies based on success
—Spontaneous activity
—Peer teaching
—Sensory-motor preparation for intellectual development
—Natural social development
—Biological basis for support of developmental needs
—Responsible freedom

ADULT ASPECTS
—Professionally educated and certified Montessori educator
—Regularly scheduled staff meetings
—On-going in-service training for auxiliary classroom personnel
—Parent education programs

ADMINISTRATIVE SUPPORT SYSTEMS
—Identifiable legally and fiscally responsible entity
—Non-discriminatory admissions policy
—Regular administrator
—Published educational policies and procedures
—Adherence to state laws and health requirements
—Membership in professional national society

In our area there is a Montessori school that has real problems. Many of the parents are dissatisfied and several have withdrawn their children.

The name "Montessori" is used by some schools which are not genuine Montessori operations. Some so-called Montessori schools lack good administration or adequate teachers. Others are failing financially for various reasons. In such situations parent dissatisfaction or staff conflict is hardly surprising.

Do not many nursery schools and kindergartens employ Montessori methods without necessarily labeling them "Montessori"?

Many do utilize some Montessori principles, activities, or materials in varying degrees.

What is the most important component of a Montessori school?

A competent, dedicated directress. Fancy facilities cannot compensate for a weak teacher, but a conscientious, capable directress can create an effective Montessori environment even in meager facilities.

The Assumption Montessori Training Course (Philadelphia, Pa.) has put the matter well:

The child, from birth, is motivated by an insatiable desire to work and to learn. While the Montessori method anticipates and accounts for that desire, it is the teacher who is responsible for its satisfaction. The Montessori teacher is essential to the success of the method. As a loving presence radiating joy and security, the teacher

becomes a link between the child and the environment
—observing, guiding, but never pressuring or imposing his
will or ideas. Fulfillment of this responsibility for the
Montessori teacher is marked in the child's progress
towards independence, concentration and ultimately, the
inner discipline that sets him free.

Can any school use the name "Montessori"?
Apparently so. The term "Montessori" is now considered generic and in the public domain. Therefore, the name
"Montessori" provides no real assurance that the Montessori approach is being employed.

*A school administrator tells me his school has no
Montessori teachers but nevertheless incorporates the best
of Montessori.*
Ask him to specify what this "best" is.

*I want my three-year-old to attend a Montessori school, but
there is none in our town. If I join with other interested
parents could we organize one?*
Groups of parents have started hundreds of successful
Montessori schools. Planning, organization, and hard work
are essential. Often such groups first go through a
study-group phase, meeting regularly to discuss Montessori
and lay the groundwork for forming a school.

*I want to set up a Montessori school. What tasks need to be
accomplished?*
Secure a suitable facility, furnish and equip it; meet all
zoning and licensing requirements; obtain and keep good
teachers and other staff; enroll sufficient children; develop
and maintain constructive parent involvement; manage
financially; provide adequate supervision and administration. For further details, see "So You Want to Start a
Montessori School" in *Montessori Today,* by R. C. Orem.
The American Montessori Society, through its Associate
Affiliate Program, can supply specifics and help in many of
the needed areas. These include cost estimates, sources for
supplies, help in securing a qualified staff, consultive
personnel, suggested speakers, and support on many
levels. The following checklist provided by AMS is a useful

starting point for anyone who is considering opening a
Montessori school:

SOME CONSIDERATIONS IN STARTING A
MONTESSORI SCHOOL OR PROGRAM

A Check List

1. *Research Montessori education*
   a. read Dr. Montessori's and other pertinent books
   b. visit Montessori schools
2. *Check state and local regulations* governing the operation
   of private nurseries, kindergartens and/or day care
   centers.

3. *Investigate the locale*
   a. is there need for a Montessori school?
   b. will such a school have community support?
4. *Determine the kind of program* to be established and the
   population to be served
   a. children from middle - income and/or affluent
      families
   b. children from culturally deprived milieus
   c. cross-cultural program for multi-ethnic, mixed
      background children
   d. program primarily concerned with learning-disa-
      bility children
   e. day care program
   f. preschool only, or ongoing program

5. *Choose the kind of organization*
   a. non-profit establishment operated by a parent
      board
   b. non-profit establishment operated by a board, not
      necessarily parents
   c. non-profit establishment operated by a Montes-
      sori teacher
   d. profit-making establishment operated by a Mon-
      tessori teacher

    e. profit-making establishment operated by an owner, partnership or corporation

6. *Obtain legal advice* as to
   a. incorporation and registration of the organization
   b. writing and effectuating a constitution and by-laws
   c. officers and/or board of directors
   d. fulfilling state and local requirements
   e. establishing an appropriate, legally responsible organization

7. *Consider finances*
   a. Initial outlay should include:
      1. adequate facilities (purchased or rented) fulfilling local requirements as to space, fire, health regulations and Montessori needs
      2. renovations (which may require an architect)
      3. child-oriented furnishings
      4. Montessori learning apparatus
      5. practical life equipment
      6. outdoor facilities and equipment
   b. Operating budget should include:
      1. rent or mortgage payments
      2. interest on loans
      3. maintenance
      4. depreciation
      5. salaries: teacher, assistant, janitorial services, administrator, secretary (unless the two last are volunteered)
      6. insurance, benefits, etc.
      7. AMS affiliation and AMS consultation fee
      8. consumable materials
      9. contingency fund
   c. Establish tuition and any other fees
   d. Plan ways of augmenting income (if needed)

8. *Select site*
    a. Check zoning restrictions
    b. Consider accessibility

9. *Hire a qualified Montessori teacher* who fulfills local requirements

10. *Establish good public relations*
    a. Recruit students through
        1. holding public meetings, workshops demonstrations, slide/film showings
        2. advertising (newspapers, TV, radio)
        3. talks/presentations at colleges, clubs, etc.
        4. one-to-one contacts
    b. Be accessible
        1. telephone
        2. interviews
        3. prompt response to letters
        4. opportunities to meet teachers and view environment

11. *Establish registration procedures*
    a. Accept children on predetermined, known, objective basis
    b. Balance classes by age and sex distribution
    c. Schedule children into sessions
    d. Require a deposit with registration
    e. Plan orientation period for new children

12. *Educate parents*
    a. class observation
    b. open houses
    c. parent study groups
    d. parent conferences

13. *Program for growth and continuity*
    a. Establish sound administrative policies
    b. Plan in advance for
        1. financial security
        2. curriculum development and improvement

    c. Become known in the community
      1. visit other schools
      2. become acquainted with teachers in public and traditional schools
      3. participate in public educational events
    d. Be open to growth via
      1. professional memberships
      2. professional consultation
      3. continued teacher, administrator and board education

Is Montessori mainly for children in the upper socioeconomic classes?

Montessori in the U. S. has tended to have the image of a white, suburban "middle-class and above" phenomenon, but an increasing number of children from diverse ethnic, racial, socioeconomic, and "special" backgrounds attend Montessori schools. There are now an increasing number of Montessori programs beamed specifically to urban "disadvantaged" children.

Frankly, Montessori does not have a very good reputation in some areas.

It takes but one poorly run Montessori school to create parental dissatisfaction, which may turn into disillusionment with Montessori in general.

Montessori teachers and schools vary considerably in their interpretation and application of Montessori. Is there such a thing as "pure" Montessori?

Whether they are American Montessori Society (AMS), Association Montessori Internationale (AMI), affiliated with another organization, or "independent," there is often great variation between Montessori schools and among teachers within the same school. Much of this variation is attributable to differences in teacher personality, training, and experience, as well as differences in types of students served and physical facilities. Montessori is not standardized, but the written works by Montessori undoubtedly contain the most authentic statements on her philosophy and method.

Why are there not more Montessori schools for older children in this country?

Many parents who would like to continue their child's Montessori education after age five find that a school is not available. There are several reasons for this: newness of the Montessori renaissance; difficulty in meeting state licensing requirements; scarcity of qualified teachers; limited Montessori teacher-training opportunities for those who want to teach older children; cost factors.

Many Montessori schools are beginning to institute higher-level classes, and teacher-training opportunities for those higher levels are expanding in America. The teacher supply-and-demand situation has brightened.

When was the first Montessori school opened in the United States?

It was opened in 1912 in Tarrytown, N. Y., by Anne E. George, who translated *The Montessori Method* into English and was Montessori's first American pupil. Whitby School (Greenwich, Conn.), the first of the "new wave" of Montessori schools in the U. S., was founded in 1958.

MONTESSORI'S WRITINGS

What writings of Dr. Montessori are available in English?

Approximately two dozen of her books and pamphlets, and numerous articles, have been translated into English. Write to the American Montessori Society (175 Fifth Avenue, New York, N. Y. 10010) for a price list.

Selected Publications by Dr. Maria Montessori

1. *The Montessori Method: Scientific Pedagogy as Applied to Child Education in "The Children's Houses,"* 1912.
2. *Pedagogical Anthropology*, 1913.
3. *Dr. Montessori's Own Handbook*, 1914.
4. *The Advanced Montessori Method. Vol. I: Spontaneous Activity in Education*, 1917.
5. *The Advanced Montessori Method. Vol. II: The Montessori Elementary Material*, 1917.

6. *The Child and the Church: Essays on the Religious Education of Children and the Training of Character,* 1929.
7. *The Mass Explained to Children,* 1933.
8. *Peace and Education,* 1948.
9. *Reconstruction in Education,* 1948.
10. *The "Erdkinder" and the Functions of the University: The Reform of Education During and After Adolescence,* no date given.
11. *The Formation of Man,* 1955.
12. *To Educate the Human Potential,* 1956.
13. *The Discovery of the Child: Revised and Enlarged Edition of "The Montessori Method,"* 1958.
14. *The Secret of Childhood,* 1959.
15. *Education for a New World,* 1959.
16. *The Child,* 1961.
17. *What You Should Know About Your Child,* 1961.
18. *The Absorbent Mind,* 1961.
19. *Maria Montessori Introducing the Child,* no date given.
20. *The Child in the Family,* 1970.

What can I read to learn more about Montessori?
For a start, try the following, all edited by R. C. Orem, and available in both cloth and soft-cover editions:

1. *A Montessori Handbook,* 1965
2. *Montessori for the Disadvantaged,* 1967
3. *Montessori and the Special Child,* 1969
4. *The Children's House Parent/Teacher Guide to Montessori* (with Ken Edelson), 1970
5. *American Montessori Manual* (with George Stevens), 1970
6. *Montessori Today,* 1971

Each of the above books contains extensive references and bibliographies concerning Montessori and related developments. Additional books by and about Montessori are available from many libraries, bookstores, and Montessori societies.

What, in your opinion, is Montessori's most important book?

It is hardly possible to select *the* most important book. They vary in subject matter, size, etc. *The Montessori Method*, first published in English in 1912 (and since reprinted by several publishers), is the classic statement of her "scientific pedagogy." *The Absorbent Mind*, published nearly forty years later, contains her most lucid discussion of the psychology of early childhood. *The Discovery of the Child* (1948) is a revision of *The Montessori Method* reflecting her experience in India.

What is the significance of THE MONTESSORI METHOD?

The Montessori Method: Scientific Pedagogy as Applied to Child Education in "The Children's Houses" is the English translation (published in 1912) of *Il Metodo della Pedagogia Scientifica applicato all' educazione infantile nelle Case dei Bambini*. The Italian version of the book was originally published in 1909. *The Montessori Method* describes the origins, principles, implementation, and results of her scientific pedagogy. The book, a best-seller in the United States before World War I, has been translated into more than a score of languages, and is the most famous of all her books.

I have been reading one of Montessori's books, and some of the material seems antiquated to me.

A number of Montessori's early books, written over half a century ago, have been reprinted in recent years. Parts of some of these books, such as the chapter on diet in the original *Montessori Method*, are obsolete, if charming. Also, Montessori's style, while often quite penetrating, is sometimes verbose by today's standards. For a comprehensive analysis of the insights to be found in Montessori's written work, the reader is referred to *American Montessori Manual*.

I find some repetitiveness in Montessori's writings.

There is considerable overlapping. For example, a number of Montessori's later published works are restatements or revisions of earlier material. *The Discovery of the Child*, for example, is basically a rephrasing of her earlier and best-known work, *The Montessori Method*.

I sometimes find Montessori's vocabulary a little confusing.

There is an element of confusion. Montessori's "system" and her terminology were dynamic, not closed or completed. She frequently modified her vocabulary from one book to the next. To cite but one example, the reader may find the terms "inner force," "constructive energy," "psychic energy," and "psychic power" used interchangeably in her books. The quality of the translation from Italian to English is also a factor.

MOTIVATION

Why was Montessori opposed to the use of prizes and punishments in education?

She referred to prizes as "trifling attractions" and to punishments as "petty ills," considering both "degrading to body and spirit."

Furthermore, "the prize and the punishment are incentives toward unnatural or forced effort, and, therefore we certainly cannot speak of the natural development of the child in connection with them."

MOVEMENT IN EDUCATION

Why are Montessori children often on the floor?

Because they want to be. They are free to move about and to spread their work upon the floor. When the floor is not carpeted, each child uses his own little carpet.

In a letter to the author, Ms. Fleta Garsaud, administrator of the Children's House (New Orleans, La.), describes the school's new "gym room."

This past summer we realized a dream. We had a 1000 sq. ft. "gym room" for large-muscle activity constructed. There is a teacher in this room at all times, and the children are free to use the climbing rope, basketball goal, chinning bar and rings, bean bags, balls and scooter-boards. (All of this equipment is child-scaled.) There is also an area for large kindergarten-type blocks where the children build everything from houses to trains. There are mats for tumbling and rolling, and, of course, a phonograph for rhythm games and dances. We also use this room for showing movies with our 16 mm projector.

Will my child's coordination be improved in a Montessori program?

Very likely it will be. One-third of the Montessori method is devoted to what she termed "motor education," which helps develop muscular coordination.

MYSTICAL ELEMENT

I detect a strong mystical element in Montessori's work.

Various authors have referred to the "mystic," "pseudo-mystic," "religious," or "spiritual" elements in Montessori. While her methodological writings reflect Montessori as the clinician and scientific pedagogue, the mystical materials reflect her as the spiritual teacher whose mission is to prepare the environment for the new child—the little messiah who will regenerate man.

"NEW EDUCATION"

What will be the source of the "new education" according to Montessori?

" . . . the study of the individual" through the "observation of *free* children by trained observers."

NORMALIZED CHILD

What did Montessori mean by the term "normalized child"?

A child who has achieved self-discipline and psychic stability through work in freedom. Such a child reflects the harmonious development fostered by creative experiences in a prepared environment.

What is a "deviated child"?

A child whose development has been thwarted or

distorted by negative factors in his environment. Such a child lacks mastery of himself and his environment.

OPPOSITION TO MONTESSORI

Why are so many educators overtly or covertly opposed to Montessori?

Many lack a clear understanding of her theory and practice, having neither studied her works nor observed in Montessori schools. The American educational establishment, as is often true of institutions, is not noted for openness to change. The Montessori method, running counter to much that is practiced in traditional education, is perceived as a threat.

I am taking a university course in early-childhood education, and the professor always seems to be "knocking" Montessori.

Let's be candid. Many educators who have a vested interest in maintaining the status quo, for reasons of prestige, power, and "purse," may be more interested in promoting their own views than in impartial examination of issues. On the positive side, a number of colleges and universities are establishing one or more Montessori courses for undergraduate or graduate credit.

ORDER

Montessori places such a great deal of emphasis upon order. Doesn't she overdo its importance?

Montessori believes that the child's *love of order* is something more than what we adults mean by the words. "It is a vital need at a certain age, in which disorder is painful and is felt as a wound in the depths of the soul, so that the child might say, 'I cannot *live* unless I have order about me.' It is indeed a question of life and death."

What is the "sensitive period for order"?

The period from age one to about three and one-half, when the child is defining himself in relation to his environment and acquiring a sense of order—thus the vital importance of environmental order during this time. Says Montessori, "It is the order in which the objects in the environment are kept which teaches the child the idea of order."

OUTDOORS

Do Montessori children have outdoor activities?
Montessori children typically have daily outdoor activities—often more extensive than their public school counterparts. There are nature hikes, gardening, group games, play on equipment, etc. Some Montessori schools have large grounds, with animals, fruit trees, and outbuildings. There are practical life exercises for the outdoors: raking, weeding, etc.

Do Montessori children go on field trips?
Montessori schools schedule trips to museums, parks, businesses, and other historical, cultural, and educational sites.

PLAY

I read somewhere that play is not allowed in Montessori. Is this true?
Montessori children have ample opportunities for play.

PRACTICAL LIFE EXERCISES

What are "practical life exercises"?
Tasks to teach the child care of himself (grooming, dressing, shining shoes, etc.) and care of the environment both indoors (washing, sweeping, table setting, etc.) and outdoors (weeding, raking, etc.). These tasks encourage in the child the growth of independence and a sense of responsibility for order in his surroundings.

PRACTICE

Why was Montessori so concerned with the role of practice in education?

According to Montessori, "What strengthens any developing power is practice, and practice is still needed after the basic power has been attained."

PREPARED ENVIRONMENT

What is the "prepared environment"?
A room or rooms with child-sized, functional furnishings and Montessori didactic equipment staffed with a directress to foster auto-education. There should also be adequate grounds for outdoor activities.

PROGRAMMED INSTRUCTION

The organization of the Montessori method reminds me of programmed instruction.
Certain principles are inherent in both. For example: specifying goals in advance, dealing with one skill or concept at a time, presenting material one step at a time, in a specific sequence; gaining mastery of one skill or concept before introducing something new; relating a new skill or concept to that which has already been learned; provision of sufficient practice; provision of reinforcement, etc.

The manner in which Montessori exercises are divided into small, step-by-step tasks is too artificial. A child does not always learn by such steps.
Montessori was well aware that children employ various methods and styles of learning, and designed her system accordingly. Speaking of the traditional teacher, she says: "The teacher considers that she must lead the child from the easy to the difficult, from simple to complex, by gradual steps, whereas the child may go from the difficult to the easy, and make great strides."

PUBLIC EDUCATION AND MONTESSORI

Are public educators putting Montessori into the schools? Is Montessori "catching on" in the public schools?
Some public school systems are instituting pilot Montessori classes and offering in-service training in Montessori

principles to teachers. It remains for a large public school system to institute Montessori on a broad scale.

Under Title III of the Elementary and Secondary Education Act, projects designed to demonstrate worthwhile innovations in educational practice through exemplary programs can be funded. These are PACE projects. The acronym stands for Projects to Advance Creativity in Education. In Washington, D.C., such a project is the Montessori Preschool at the John Burroughs Elementary School, directed by Mrs. Doris Hundley.

In the United States, Montessori has been confined largely to preschool classes in private schools or tuition schools purposely organized for Montessori. This has given Montessori a preschool, private school image. Yet, Montessori is applicable at all grade levels and in a wide variety of settings. To demonstrate the contribution that the Montessori method can make to public education, the principal, faculty, and parents of John Burroughs Elementary School began in 1971–72 the Montessori program at John Burroughs.

The success of the project is evidenced in the participating children: self-confidence, self-discipline, independence, readiness to learn. The project is yielding an alternative model for preschool programs which could be implemented throughout the school system. There are two half-day classes of twenty children each, directed by a Montessori teacher and aide. Hopefully, Montessori will be extended into the elementary grades.

I am a public school teacher and am interested in applying Montessori in my classroom. What can I do?

You can apply at least some of the Montessori principles and utilize certain Montessori-oriented materials and exercises. For suggestions concerning specific applications, read Montessori books, visit a Montessori school and talk with the teachers; attend Montessori conferences and workshops; take some Montessori teacher training, if possible.

The staff of the Staten Island Montessori School (Staten Island, N.Y.) conducts a basic early-childhood-training workshop series on the philosophy of designing a total learning environment, and the role of the teacher in a preschool classroom. These weekend workshops are open to teachers of public schools, private schools, and day care centers throughout the Tri-State area. This basic workshop series is followed by more intensively focused weekend seminars, e.g., language arts, math, art, etc. This program is administered by Nina Liebman and utilizes the talents of Marlene Barron, Judith Fritzsche, Virginia Scanlon, Jacqueline Wexler, and Stephanie Whalen.

As a result of the success of these training services Ms. Barron now provides a consultation service and in-service training program for day care centers and residential institutions, providing on-site training in pedagogical theory, observation skills, staff and parent communication, and environment and materials design. The communication training is run in conjunction with The Center for Changing and Learning, Dr. George DeLeon, Director.

Mrs. Mary Los Banos, directress of the Children's House in Pearl City, Hawaii, teaches a course, "Individualizing Instruction in the Elementary School," for Oahu educators. The Church College of Hawaii grants three credits for the course. The Children's House provides an atmosphere conducive to understanding the role of a teacher in a flexible environment (Montessori) designed to meet the needs of the individual child. Topics include: grouping and scheduling strategies; physical facilities—arrangement and care; making individualized teaching materials (sensorial, math, reading, science, etc.); observation; diagnostic-prescriptive teaching; and reporting child's progress to parents. One outcome of the course is an understanding of how features of the Montessori approach can be used in public school classrooms.

READING

Did Montessori emphasize early reading?

Montessori did not consider "early reading" an objective of her method. Rather, many children demonstrated that, when exposed to systematic motor, sensory, and language activities in the prepared environment, they would readily learn to read before age six. See "Montessori and Early Learning" in *The Case for Early Reading* by G. L. Stevens and R. C. Orem.

REPETITION

Did Montessori believe that repetition is natural for the young learner?

She notes that "little children from three and a half years old have repeated the exercise with the cylinders up to forty times without losing interest in it," and concludes that "the normal child always repeats the exercise with growing interest."

What function does repetition serve in the learning process of the child?

Montessori speaks of the child's "love of repetition," and notes that "to have learned something is for the child a starting-point; when he has learned, then he begins to get enjoyment from the repetition of the exercise."

Even after the child has attained proficiency in a particular exercise he may continue to practice. "He repeats what he has learned an indefinite number of times, with evident satisfaction; he enjoys doing things, because in this he is developing his power."

RESEARCH

What aspects of Montessori warrant research?

Research possibilities in Montessori are virtually unlimited. A few of the many aspects of Montessori that warrant further study and reporting include: teacher training, sensory education, language learning, cognitive development, inner motivation, and personality development. Under the general headings of Teacher, Child, Environment, and Learning Process there are literally dozens of topics needing further exploration.

For example, although Montessori discussed the importance of "sensitive periods" in the child's development, definitive work on the subject remains to be done. What are the characteristics and functions of each of the sensitive periods? What are the variations in onset and duration of the various sensitive periods in different individuals, and how may these periods be best utilized in the educational process?

Montessori has provided us with useful beginnings but we must now go beyond her pioneering experiments.

Have the long-term effects of Montessori education upon individuals been researched?

To the editor's best knowledge, not a single major longitudinal study of such effects (covering, say, twenty years) has been done in this country or abroad. (For that matter, long-term research on other educational approaches is also lacking.) Such research is difficult and expensive, but obviously very much needed.

Where can I obtain funding for Montessori research and development?

High-quality proposals should be submitted to appropriate government agencies and to foundations. Some Montessori groups also raise funds from individuals, businesses, and other organizations and institutions in the community.

SENSITIVE PERIODS

What are "sensitive periods"?

Periodic sensibilities characteristic of creatures in process of development. According to Montessori, "At certain periods in life there exist possibilities of making mental acquisitions which are no longer possible at other ages." During these periods, the child demonstrates unusual capability for acquiring a particular skill and degree of competence.

What is an example of a sensitive period?
The sensitive period for learning to write is between three and a half and four and a half.

Some other sensitive periods and their approximate ranges are: precise movement and coordination (two and a half to four); acquiring a sense of order (one to three and a half); learning to read (four to five).

Why are sensitive periods important?
As Montessori has said, "It is during the sensitive period that a function can be more perfectly established, or an ability can be acquired in a more perfect manner."

Are the child's sensitive periods transitory?
Yes. Once past, according to Montessori, they cannot be recaptured—thus, the importance of utilizing them educationally.

Montessori spoke of various periods in the development of the individual. Is there a most-important period?
Says Montessori: "From 0 to 6 is the most important part of life, and this applies to character development also."

Who discovered sensitive periods in animals? In humans?
Says Montessori:

> It was the Dutch scientist, Hugo deVries, who discovered the existence of sensitive periods in animal life, but we ourselves, in our schools and by observing the life of children in their families, were the first to discover the sensitive periods of infancy, and to make use of them from the standpoint of education.

SENSORY EDUCATION

What is Montessori sensory education?
The sensory materials and exercises present qualities such as color, form, dimension, sound, texture, etc., in a

graded, tangible manner enabling the child to analyze and classify these qualities. Says Montessori:

> We cannot create observers by saying, *observe,* but by giving them the power and the means for this *observation:* these means are procured through education of the senses.

What is the purpose of sensory education according to Montessori?

> It is exactly in the repetition of the exercises that the education of the senses consists: the aim of the exercises is not that the child shall *know* colors, forms and the different qualities of objects, but that he refine his senses through an exercise of attention, of comparison, of judgment.

SHARING

In Montessori there is not enough emphasis upon sharing. Children need to be taught to share.

Sharing in the traditional nursery or kindergarten is too often "rotten coercion." In Montessori schools, children learn to share—in the use of the materials, for example—but they also learn to share through service to others. Montessori children, in short, learn to *share themselves,* helping each other. Interest in the possession of objects as an end in itself, the "longing to possess," is transformed into interest in objects as means to knowledge and enlightenment.

SOCIAL DEVELOPMENT

Isn't there too little emphasis upon group work and "getting along with others" in Montessori? Do children participate in any group activities for a sense of togetherness? Didn't Montessori stress individualism too much?

Some misinformed critics speak of a lack of opportunity for socialization in Montessori education. Actually, the

Montessori environment offers far more opportunity for genuinely constructive socialization than the traditional classrooms. In the former, competitiveness is deemphasized while cooperation is fostered. The prepared environment is a miniature society with each child developing awareness of the "collective interest" and contributing to what Montessori termed "cohesion in the social unit." There are numerous indoor and outdoor group activities, but the child is not forced to participate if his interests lie elsewhere at a given moment.

What did Montessori mean by "cohesion in the social unit"?

Cooperation and concern for the group welfare shown by children helping each other in the upgraded prepared environment. In this noncompetitive atmosphere, children admire the success of their peers.

SOURCES OF INFORMATION ON MONTESSORI

How can I find out more about the Montessori method?

Read books by and about Montessori. Visit Montessori schools. Join a Montessori study group. Organize one if none is available locally. Attend Montessori lectures, conferences, or seminars. Enroll in a Montessori course.

Some of the most productive Montessori seminars experienced by the editor are sponsored by the Universal Montessori Teachers Association and Montessori Teachers Training Center. Says Mrs. Marlow Muldoon:

The Universal Montessori Teachers Association and Montessori Teachers Training Center was formed for the purpose of educating teachers, professors, and assistant teachers in the Montessori philosophy and technique. We are interested in spreading knowledge of the Montessori method to the college and university level. Many educators today feel that the Montessori method is outmoded and extreme. We hope to show the educators that they can have the latest in educational materials and technique as well as the Montessori method of education. We feel that this combination assures the child of developing his highest potential without pressure.

For further information, write to Mrs. Muldoon at the Montessori School of Dallas, 5608 Northaven Rd., Dallas, Texas 75234. The seminars are held in various sites in the United States, and abroad.

How can I find out more about the Montessori movement?
For information, write to the American Montessori Society (AMS), the Association Montessori Internationale (AMI), the International Association of Progressive Montessorians (IAPM), the Universal Montessori Teachers' Association (UMTA), or to other Montessori organizations at the regional, state, or local level. Some of them publish newsletters periodically for members, sponsor public meetings, and provide speakers for interested groups.

What is AMS?
Organized in 1960, the American Montessori Society (AMS) is a national, nonprofit, tax-exempt organization dedicated to promoting better education for all children through teaching strategies consistent with the Montessori system and the incorporation of the Montessori approach into the framework of American Education. Ms. Cleo Monson is the National Director.

AMS services include: consultation program to member schools; teacher training; AMS publications; literature, materials, and information centers; research assistance; scholarship aid; annual seminar/conference and workshops.

What is AMI?
The Association Montessori Internationale (AMI) was established in 1929 by Dr. Maria Montessori and Mario M. Montessori, her son, who continues to direct it. It is supported by distinguished scholars and statesmen all over the world. The AMI is the recognized international

authority on Montessori education and directs studies in affiliated teacher-training institutions on four continents. During its long history the AMI has fostered the growth and development of Montessori educational practices and standards through active work with member schools, teachers, and educators.

Yearly international study conferences of the AMI have served as important milestones in the development of new practices and the exchange of insights which have grown out of the application of Montessori to widely differing lands and cultures.

What is IAPM?

In 1969 Sister Angela Aguilcra, an active Montessorian for more than twenty years in Spain and England, and Grace McEntee, an educator for more than twenty years and trained in Montessori by Sister Angela, officially formed the International Association of Progressive Montessorians in New York City. Sister Angela is the international president and Grace McEntee is the president-in-America. The association has member schools in Britain, France, Spain, Japan, South America, and the United States. In the United States, there are member schools in New York City; Amarillo, Texas; Midland, Texas; Seattle, Washington; Vista, California; and Santa Fe, New Mexico.

The association has established standards for teacher training and for issuing diplomas. The top part of the diploma is filled out upon successful completion of the training course. The bottom part is completed after one successful year of teaching and is signed by the director of the course and by the principal of the school in which the trainee taught for the first year.

The IAPM insignia has been registered both with the United States and Britain. The symbol represents the philosophy of the Progressive Montessorians breaking through the confining rigidity of traditional education and freeing the child to reach his own greatest potential.

The IAPM is dedicated to providing an organized, academic approach to Montessori education, utilizing the newest innovations of modern teaching techniques in accordance with Montessori principles and practices. For further details write to IAPM, Box 2381, Santa Fe, New Mexico 87501.

What is UMTA?

One important purpose of the Universal Montessori Teachers' Association is the unity of all Montessorians through conferences, seminars and other training; research; publications and other communications. For information write to UMTA, P.O. Box 30533, Dallas, Texas 75230.

Are there other Montessori organizations?

There are local, city, state, regional, national, and international Montessori organizations of varying size and significance.

The Illinois Montessori Society, Box 735, Oak Park, Ill. 60303, is one of several groups which can provide helpful information on other groups.

Sherwood Montessori Schools, with central offices in St. Louis, Mo., operates eleven units, in addition to Montessori camps which are extending the Montessori principles into a summer day camp setting.

Robert Morris, administrator of Sherwood Montessori Schools, has identified a variety of informal and formal ways an individual can pursue the study of Montessori:

    a. a program of reading in texts by, and about, Montessori

    b. for Montessori parents, and other persons: study groups, workshops, and seminars sponsored by Montessori societies, and schools, colleges, and universities; also, observations and conferences

    c. Montessori correspondence courses

    d. nine-month residence course, in U.S. or abroad

    e. Montessori training in conjunction with undergraduate degree

    f. Montessori training in conjunction with Master's program

    g. other courses of various types and length

The editor has found Mr. Morris to be knowledgeable in the many phases of Montessori and ready to share his information. Readers with any questions may contact him at Sherwood Montessori Schools, Central Office, 12292 Clayton Road, St. Louis, Mo. 63131.

There are many opportunities for parent education in Montessori. The following are but three examples:

1. The Edwardsville (Ill.) Montessori Society conducts a one-day workshop for parents. Topics include:

Developmental Patterns in the Young Child—the sequence of development in the child from birth through age six: motor, sensory, emotional, mental.

Preparing an Environment in Your Home—decorating and furnishing a child's room, etc.

Activities at Home—suggestions and guidelines for things to do with the child which are suitable for the home, informal, and reinforce Montessori classroom experience.

Staff from the Children's House: A Montessori Child Development Center (Edwardsville, Ill.) including Assistant Directress, Beth McGivern, lead the discussions. A morning coffee break, lunch and question-and-answer session make for an enjoyable day.

The Society also conducts a parent workshop: Sharing the Holidays with Young Children. Topics include:

All That Glitters Is Not Gold: How to Buy Toys That a Child Will Really Enjoy

The Holly and the Ivy: Holiday Activities and Traditions

You Can't Judge a Book (or a Record) Just by Its Cover

2. Each fall and most springs the Westshore Montessori School (Fairfax Park, Ohio) sponsors five-week Parent-Study Groups which are free and open to the community. Course I covers such topics as The Normalized Child, Preparing the Environment for the Child, Sensitive Periods of the Child, The Work of the Child, and Freedom and Discipline for the Child. Course II is for people who have taken Course I and covers the basic rationale, presentations, and practice with the materials in Practical Life, Sensorial, Language, Math, and the Cultural Subjects.

The most recent training course, Parent-Toddler Classes, was aimed at parents of one-and-a-half- to two-and-a-half-year-olds and designed to help parents understand and put Montessori principles into their homes before the child enters school. Parents meet one evening a week for discussions centering around *The Secret of Childhood,* and bring their child to the classroom for one and a half hours on Saturday mornings. This enables the parents to observe their children in an environment prepared for them. This is the only course for which there is tuition: $20.00 for the five weeks. Size is limited to eight families.

3. The Purdue University Office of Continuing Education began offering in 1971 a noncredit course, Montessori Methods for Teachers and Parents, at the Calumet Campus (Hammond, Ind.). The course meets for ten Monday-night sessions, each two hours in length.

The aims of this course are to develop an awareness of what actually takes place in a Montessori school and to share the wealth of knowledge concerning the child which Maria Montessori discovered and developed. Participants are exposed to actual Montessori environments and the philosophy of the Montessori method is explained.

Miss Claire Therrieu, Administrator-Directress of the Montessori Children's Schoolhouse in Hammond, Indiana, teaches the course.

The following syllabus lists the topic(s) of each of the ten sessions:

1. Introduction to Montessori (biographical information)
2. Practical Life Exercises
3. The Sensorial Apparatus
4. Montessori Environment (at school)
5. Discussion of Montessori Environment
6. Development of Language
7. Observation of Children
8. Science and Geography (discussion of observation)
9. Math
10. Place of Music and Art—Summary and Discussion

Is there available a summary of Montessori's views on education?

The American Montessori Manual (Orem and Stevens) describes more than four hundred Montessori concepts related to education. See the extensive AMS price list of publications.

Is there available a glossary of Montessori terms?

The American Montessori Manual contains the most comprehensive one: a cross-referenced glossary containing more than three hundred terms used by Montessori in her published works.

How can I contact other persons interested in Montessori?

Visit Montessori schools; attend Montessori conferences; join a Montessori organization or study group.

How can I contact Montessori schools in my area?

Check the Yellow Pages of your telephone directory. AMS and AMI publish lists of affiliated schools. *Children's House* magazine publishes a directory in each issue.

SPECIAL EDUCATION; RETARDED CHILDREN

Is the Montessori method mainly for "special" children such as the retarded?

No. For example, a survey conducted by the editor revealed that only 10 percent of children enrolled in Montessori schools at that time were "special" children. Some Montessori schools enroll a few special children or have a class for such children, and there are a few Montessori schools specifically for these children. There are other Montessori schools that enroll no special children.

Will prolonged exposure to the Montessori method enable a deficient child to function at the normal child's level?

Although the Montessori method will help the deficient child to achieve his potential, whatever it may be, she notes that "the abyss between inferior mentality of the deficient child and that of the normal brain can never be bridged if the normal child has reached his full development."

Is Montessori helpful in teaching the deaf?

Montessori does have applications to deaf education, although she did not develop her methods with the education of the deaf as a primary consideration. It is interesting to note that Alexander Graham Bell, a pioneer in deaf education, was an early proponent of the Montessori method and officer of the Montessori Society of America.

STRUCTURE

I've heard that Montessori is too structured—that there is too much control. Isn't there too much emphasis upon orderliness?

Montessori auto-education provides the child an environment that encourages self-development. Within reasonable limits, he is free to move about, talk, choose his work, and follow his own schedule of activities. Unfortunately, it is true that there are some directresses whose implementation of the Montessori approach is narrow or rigid.

TEACHER TRAINING

What does Montessori teacher training involve?

A typical training course, approximately a year in length, consists of lectures on Montessori theory and practice, demonstrations, materials laboratory, observation at schools, and supervised internship (similar to practice teaching). See Section IV.

There are many variations among courses in terms of content, organization, length, schedule, requirements, etc. AMS and AMI approve a number of courses. Some courses are affiliated with a college or university, and there are even correspondence courses.

> The St. Nicholas Montessori Training Centre located at 22-24 Princes Gate, London S.W. 7, England, offers several types of Montessori training, including correspondence courses. Various options are available regarding schedule, length, activities, credit, and certificate. Co-principals Margaret Homfray and Phoebe Child were both trained by Maria Montessori in London and Rome, and may be contacted for further information at the above address.

What is required academically for admission to Montessori teacher training?

In the U.S., a bachelor's degree is often (but not necessarily) required of those applying for admission to Montessori teacher-training programs.

What does Montessori teacher training cost?

Tuition for an intensive one-year course may cost approximately $1,500. This figure varies considerably. The trainee will also likely pay for materials, transportation, and, if from out of town, room and board.

> The Central Harlem Association of Montessori Parents (CHAMP) has a Montessori teacher-training project which is attempting to make such training available to persons who might otherwise not have

access to it because of financial reasons or lack of formal education.

How selective are Montessori training programs? Can anyone enroll?

Some training programs screen rather rigorously, especially if applicants exceed the facilities, but many courses are rather free-wheeling in enrollment.

How about the abbreviated Montessori courses?

Some teacher trainees who conduct shorter Montessori courses claim that Montessori teacher training can indeed be compressed without loss of quality. In some training courses, a great amount of time is spent by each trainee in listening to lectures on the Montessori exercises and then laboriously preparing from lecture notes a set of manuals for the various types of Montessori exercises. In other courses, most of this material is duplicated and given to the trainees for assembling into manuals.

Is one Montessori teacher as effective as another if both have taken the same training?

Like all teachers, Montessori teachers vary greatly—one could say enormously—in dedication and competence. Some, even though they have completed a training course, lack the necessary qualities to function very effectively as a directress.

Why do many persons who already have teacher certification and years of teaching experience choose to take Montessori teacher training?

Motives are varied. Many trainees have told the author that they sense in Montessori what they have been seeking for years. They often express dissatisfaction with their earlier educational training and with their experience in public schools.

Some see in Montessori a means of escaping a dissatisfying classroom situation, or of gaining added prestige and marketability as a teacher.

Some say they believe Montessori offers them the opportunity to be a teacher in the real sense of the word, for perhaps the first time.

TOYS

Was Montessori opposed to toys in her method?

For toys, Montessori would substitute "houses," and land on which children "can work with small tools." Instead of dolls, she suggests "real other children and a social life in which they can act for themselves." She rates toys as "better than nothing," but adds that "it is significant that the child quickly tires of toys and wants new ones." Although her school contained "some really wonderful toys," she observed that "the children never chose them." The Montessori method, in lieu of doll houses, play kitchens, toy animals, etc., "seeks to give all this to the child in reality—making him an actor in a living scene." She sought to place "real articles" at the child's disposal, to be touched and handled. For a "balanced diet of toys," see the toy guide published by the Illinois Montessori Society.

Betty Lewis is directress of one of the most successful Montessori schools in the Midwest: the Johnson County Pre-School and Kindergarten (Overland Park, Kansas). The following material is gleaned from the school's newsletter to parents:

Many of you ask each year about gifts for your children. We would like to offer the following suggestions:

TOYS:

A well-selected toy can help your child develop physically, intellectually, socially, emotionally or creatively.

Preschool children need toys which provide opportunities for squeezing, pulling, pushing, stacking, pounding, lifting, balancing, throwing, catching, bouncing, dragging, steering, carrying, climbing, rolling, taking apart, putting together, cuddling, talking to, listening to, creating with and thinking.

Following are some suggestions—especially for pre-schoolers:

1. Riding toys without pedals (to age 3)
2. Riding toys with pedals (3 yrs. up)
3. Wagons
4. Low climbers
5. Talking telephone
6. Dolls
7. Large and small balls
8. Simple puzzles
9. Housekeeping toys
10. Blocks
11. Water toys
12. Tinkertoy and Lincoln Logs (the 4-6 yr. old loves to build)
13. Small animals, people, vehicles and buildings
14. Modeling clay and crayons, paints, paper, paste and scissors
15. Good books and records
16. Puppets
17. Musical instruments
18. Science activities, such as a plant for the child to observe and take care of, magnets and objects, a prism, scale, ant colony, fish, bird or squirrel feeder outside child's window, or magnifying glass
19. Large chalkboard
20. Record player

More suggestions:

Stringing or gluing macaroni and other safe household items.

Large and small cardboard boxes to play in and with, or pitch a ball into.

Batting a balloon with an empty paper towel tube.

A two-by-four on a couple of bricks to balance on.

Mom and dad to play ball with or hop on one foot with.

The best modeling "dough" is made of flour, salt, water and love.

Even the best story is better heard while sitting in a soft, warm lap.

Relax and enjoy childhood with your child!

Although not a toy, a pet for a gift can easily be the most loved and important. Through the years, when I asked children what is most important to them, it is usually family, friends and pets. This is easy to understand since living beings can respond to needs and have needs. A pet can be a part of the family, and a friend, and will treat its owner as it is treated.

Be sure your child has a special shelf, drawer, or box to keep his art and other works in. Don't be the parent of the little child who asked the teacher, "Can I please hide my work at school?" When asked why, the reply was, "My mother throws everything I do away."

Your child also needs a table or desk his size where he can work with crayons, paper and so forth. You can help him set up some little boxes for each item so it can easily be kept in order. He can paste pictures on boxes so he will know where each item belongs.

Remember, the home is the greatest educational institution in the world and a child's parents are the most important teachers he will ever have.

The best "toys" will probably be those that are made rather than store bought.

Children enjoy using mother's real kitchen "tools" to measure, stir, bake, clean up, etc. Then there are dad's hand tools for sanding, hammering, etc.

How about those old clothes, hats and shoes for playing dress-up.

The best puppets are those made from dad's old socks or scraps from mother's sewing.

Some of the best fun is with water and sponge, washing daddy's tires, bumper and car tag.

TRADITIONAL EDUCATION

What are some of the faults of traditional education as viewed by Montessori?

To name a few: restriction of child's activity; suppression of his spontaneity; use of external rewards and punishments; frequent interruptions; verbal "pouring-in" approach; inadequate teacher training.

Says Montessori: "The educational methods now in use proceed on lines exactly the reverse of ours."

The Montessori Schools of Omaha, Nebraska, which comprise four schools—Omaha Central Montessori School, Omaha Northwest Montessori School, Bellevue Montessori School, and Lincoln Montessori School —have published the following chart by Lynn McCormick concerning some differences often evident between Montessori and traditional kindergartens.

The goal of both Montessori and traditional kindergartens is the same: to provide learning experiences for the child. The biggest differences lie in the kind of learning experiences each school provides and the methods they use to accomplish this goal.

Montessori educators believe both differences are important because they help shape what a child learns, his work habits, and his future attitudes toward himself and the world around him.

Montessori	Traditional
emphasis on cognitive development	emphasis on social development
teacher has unobtrusive role in classroom	teacher is center of classroom as "controller"
environment and method encourage self-discipline	teacher acts as primary enforcer of discipline

mainly individual instruction	mainly group instruction
mixed age grouping	same age grouping
grouping encourages children to teach and help each other	most teaching done by teacher
child chooses own work	curriculum structured for child
child discovers own concepts from self-teaching materials	child is guided to concepts by teacher
child works as long as he wishes on chosen project	child generally allotted specific time for work
child sets own learning pace	instruction pace usually set by group norm
child spots own errors from feedback of material	if work is corrected, errors usually pointed out by teacher
child reinforces own learning by repetition of work and internal feelings of success	learning is reinforced externally by repetition, rewards and punishment
multi-sensory materials for physical exploration	few materials for sensory development
organized program for learning care of self and environment (polishing shoes, cleaning the sink, etc.)	no organized program for self-care instruction—left primarily up to parents
child can work where he chooses, move around and talk at will (yet not disturb work of others); group work is voluntary	child usually assigned own chair; required to participate, sit still and listen during group lessons

VISITING MONTESSORI SCHOOLS

May I visit a Montessori school in session?

Most Montessori schools welcome visitors, but you

should call in advance to arrange a time when you can observe. Many Montessori schools also hold open houses to acquaint interested persons with their program.

Mrs. Marion Ragsdale of the Bucks County Montessori Society Children's Academy (Langhorne, Pa.), in a letter to the author, describes a novel form of Montessori/public high school cooperation:

Mrs. Libby Carver, instructor (psychology) at Neshaminy High School, asked me if her senior students could come to observe classes here at our Academy as part of their regular psychology course. I asked how many students were involved and she said "about 200" at which I flippantly remarked that it would be easier to take *our* students to the high school. So that's what happened, and we have done it three times: transported furniture (even a rug from our classroom floor), materials and students and conducted classes all day long while the senior high school kids come and go . . . It was a big job, but our students are great. You wouldn't know this wasn't what they did every day.

What are some key elements to be seen in a Montessori school?

An environment prepared with child-sized functional furnishings and Montessori didactic materials; children absorbed in self-teaching in an ungraded format, with a three-year age span; freedom of movement; disciplined activity; teacher as observer; sensory education; children working upon self-chosen tasks individually or in small groups on carpeted floor.

Founded by a group of Catholic laymen in 1961, Saint Aidan's is the oldest Montessori school in the metropolitan Washington, D.C., area. It is run cooperatively by its parents on a nonprofit, nondenominational basis as an affiliate of AMI.

Each of the Saint Aidan classrooms is directed by a teacher trained in the Montessori method. Each teacher has an assistant. There are about twenty-five students in each class, ranging in age from three to six.

Each child may choose to work with any piece of equipment which the teacher has demonstrated to him or which he feels capable of mastering from observing its use by another student. Step by step, the child develops a knowledge of shape, size, color, sound, texture; of letters, words, and number relationships; and of concepts which help him much later in his learning process.

The child may shift from activity to activity in the classroom. There are opportunities to wash, comb, dress, and polish; to count, read, write, sing, and dance. On his part he must respect the rights of others as he initiates, carries out, and completes an activity in an orderly way. Self-mastery, a sense of responsibility, and sensory-muscular training are emphasized.

As part of the regular classroom activities the children are introduced to a wide variety of musical experiences— including singing, moving to rhythms, and using simple instruments.

Art activities are integrated into the curriculum in connection with holidays, field trips, science, and social studies.

WORK

Montessori often speaks of "work" in relation to the child. What does she mean?

"Work" for the child is positive experience in the environment promoting his self-development. His "great work" is the "building" of a personality.

Montessori distinguishes between the adult's work, which culminates in an external product or service, and the child's work, which is the process of self-development. The adult has formed his personality; the child is still in the process of "auto-formation." The "playing" child is often really working to develop himself.